The Art of Algorithmic Trading: Crafting Profitable Strategies

Talvek Rynar

THE ART OF ALGORITHMIC TRADING: CRAFTING PROFITABLE STRATEGIES

First edition. September 14, 2025.

ISBN: 979-8231548293

Written by Talvek Rynar.

From Hot Takes to Hot Trades

Let me take you back to the day I rage-quit manual trading.

It was a crisp Tuesday morning. I had my overpriced coffee, three screens glowing like a NASA control room, and a "foolproof" trade setup that I found in a Reddit thread posted by someone named "StonksGuru420." What could possibly go wrong?

I hit buy.

And within twenty minutes, the market slapped me so hard I had to sit down twice.

That was the moment—the final straw, the spiritual awakening, the scene in every hero's journey where the protagonist stares into the abyss and whispers, "There's got to be a better way."

And there was: algorithmic trading.

Welcome to the Matrix (of Market Logic)

Look, if you've ever traded based on feelings, Twitter threads, or that one friend who swears he "knows a guy," you're not alone. I've been there. We all start there. But eventually, if you survive the emotional rollercoaster long enough, you realize that markets don't care about your gut feelings—they respond to data, structure, and discipline.

That's where algorithmic trading enters like a digital superhero in a hoodie and noise-canceling headphones.

I didn't grow up a math prodigy. I didn't work at a hedge fund. And I still can't pronounce "heteroscedasticity" without flinching. But what I did have was curiosity, a laptop, and the stubborn belief that there had to be a smarter way to trade.

Spoiler: There is.

And in this book, I'm going to show you how.

Why Algorithms? Because Emotions Suck at Trading

Let's get something straight—humans are irrational. Especially under pressure. We buy the top because we fear missing out. We sell the bottom because we panic. We revenge trade. We overtrade. We under-trade. Sometimes, we don't even know why we clicked the button. It just "felt right."

But machines? Machines don't care. They don't get greedy. They don't hold grudges. They follow rules. They execute with precision. And best of all—they work while you sleep.

That's the dream, right?

Algorithmic trading isn't just for quants in corner offices anymore. It's for anyone willing to learn how to turn logic into action, code into cash, and strategy into structure.

Okay, But What's Actually in This Book?

Think of this book as your algorithmic trading bootcamp, minus the yelling drill sergeant and plus some awkward jokes.

We start at square one—what is algorithmic trading, and why should you care? Then we dive into how markets actually work (spoiler: not how your TikTok feed says they do), followed by the tools you'll need to code your own trading strategies—even if you've never written a line of Python in your life.

You'll learn how to design, test, and optimize strategies with actual structure. We'll talk about how to avoid traps like overfitting, how to backtest responsibly (without cheating), and how to build bots that don't just look cool—they actually work.

Later, we'll explore advanced techniques like statistical arbitrage, sentiment analysis, and machine learning, all broken down so you won't need a PhD in math or a translator.

And yes, we'll talk about the stuff nobody likes to talk about: risk. Because blowing up your account in a blaze of glory is only fun in movies. In real life, you want to survive long enough to win.

But Wait... Coding?! Don't Panic.

I can already hear the nervous whispers: "But I'm not a programmer..."

Relax. I got you.

If you can understand basic English, you can write basic Python. I'll walk you through it like a friend who's good at explaining stuff without making you feel like an idiot. We're not building billion-dollar high-frequency trading systems here—we're building smart, sustainable, logical strategies that automate what you already try to do manually (but probably with more coffee and anxiety).

By the end, you'll not only understand what's going on under the hood—you'll enjoy it. Seriously.

A Real Talk Disclaimer

Now, let's be honest—this book is not a get-rich-quick scheme. I'm not here to sell you "the secret strategy the hedge funds don't want you to know." If you're looking for that, I hear there's a YouTube guy with a Lambo and a whiteboard waiting for you.

This book is about the craft. The process. The mindset. The thrill of turning an idea into a system, testing it, refining it, deploying it, and watching it do its thing while you eat tacos.

You will fail. You will break code. You will question your sanity. But if you stick with it, you'll build something that works because you made it work.

And that's pretty damn cool.

Who This Book Is For (Yes, You)

Whether you're:

- A frustrated day trader tired of emotional mistakes
- A developer curious about finance
- A finance nerd curious about code
- A robot sent from the future to destroy human market inefficiencies (no judgment)

...this book is for you.

You don't need to know everything—you just need to be curious enough to start, stubborn enough to keep going, and brave enough to test your ideas in the wild.

Let's Build. Let's Break. Let's Automate.

The markets are fast. Unforgiving. Ruthless. But also kind of beautiful in their chaos. Algorithmic trading gives you the power to navigate them with structure and style.

You're not just learning to trade—you're learning to engineer trades. You're not chasing setups—you're building systems. And you're not relying on luck—you're relying on logic, data, and your own brilliant brain.

So grab a coffee. Fire up your code editor. Let's build your first bot, break some bad habits, and maybe—just maybe—start trading like the legend you know you could be.

Let's go.

Chapter 1: Foundations of Algorithmic Trading

Ever tried beating the market by randomly yelling "buy!" or "sell!" like a Wall Street movie character? Spoiler: it doesn't work (we tried). Welcome to the world where computers make smarter, faster, and more emotionless decisions than any caffeine-powered trader ever could. Algorithmic trading isn't just for hoodie-wearing quants in basement lairs—it's for anyone ready to harness code to conquer chaos.

This chapter introduces the fundamentals of algorithmic trading, tracing its roots and evolution in the financial markets. It explores the core components of an algorithmic strategy, contrasts manual with automated trading, and emphasizes the central role that technology now plays in market execution and analysis.

1.1 What Is Algorithmic Trading?

Let's get one thing out of the way first: algorithmic trading is not a bunch of robots sitting in a dark server room plotting to destroy the stock market. Well, not yet anyway. If you're imagining Skynet meets Wall Street, take a breath. There's no artificial intelligence uprising—just a bunch of nerds (like me) writing code that tries to outsmart other nerds writing slightly better code. Sometimes we win. Sometimes we go back to the drawing board with a tub of ice cream and a therapy session with our Python scripts.

So, what is algorithmic trading?

At its core, algorithmic trading—also called algo trading or automated trading—is the process of using computer programs to execute trades in financial markets based on a pre-defined set of rules. These rules can be as simple as "buy this stock if it drops 2% in a day" or as complex as "analyze 38 indicators, cross-check with sentiment analysis from Twitter, throw in a lunar cycle, and go long if Mercury is in retrograde."

Okay, maybe not the astrology part. (Unless that's your edge. In which case—go nuts, but don't quote me.)

The Algorithmic Edge

Back in the day—cue nostalgic music and sepia-toned memories—trading was all about humans yelling at each other in trading pits. It was chaos, it was beautiful, and it smelled vaguely of sweat and stress. Fast forward to today, and it's mostly machines talking to other machines in nanoseconds, executing trades faster than you can blink.

The "algorithm" in algorithmic trading is just a fancy name for a set of instructions. If X happens, do Y. If not, wait for Z. It's logic, pure and simple. The complexity comes from what X, Y, and Z are, how they're defined, and how well your system adapts to ever-changing market conditions.

The "trading" part? Well, that's the easy bit. Buying low, selling high (or vice versa in short selling), but doing it with speed, precision, and ideally, no emotion.

Notice I said "ideally"? Because trust me, nothing ruins a perfectly good algorithm like a human suddenly panicking because the chart looked "weird."

Why Go Algo?

Let's be real: humans are emotional, inconsistent, and need sleep. Algorithms don't. They work 24/7 (if you let them), never get tired, never second-guess themselves, and don't need coffee to function.

Here's why so many traders—myself included—eventually go down the algo rabbit hole:

- **Speed:** Algorithms execute trades in milliseconds. You, on the other hand, have to move your mouse.
- **Discipline:** No second-guessing, no FOMO, no revenge trading. The algorithm does what it's told.
- **Backtesting:** You can test your strategy on historical data to see how it would have performed. Note: Would have. Past performance, blah blah blah, no guarantees, yada yada.
- **Scale:** You can monitor and trade dozens, even hundreds, of instruments simultaneously.

And yes, there are downsides. Bad code can lose you money faster than you can say "debug." Markets evolve. And don't even get me started on overfitting—that seductive siren that makes your backtest look amazing and your real trading account cry.

But still, if done right, algorithmic trading is like hiring a loyal employee who never sleeps and doesn't care about your ex texting you at 2 a.m. during a trading session.

Not Just for Hedge Funds Anymore

You might be thinking, "Isn't this stuff just for hedge funds and PhDs in quantum physics?"

It used to be. For years, algorithmic trading was the playground of deep-pocketed institutions with expensive infrastructure and armies of data scientists. But things have changed.

Thanks to accessible platforms like Python, free APIs, and cheap cloud computing, the barrier to entry has dropped lower than my expectations when someone tells me they're YOLOing Tesla options.

If you've got some coding chops, a solid understanding of trading principles, and a little patience (okay, maybe a lot), you can start building your own strategies from your bedroom. Or bathroom. I don't judge.

Types of Algorithmic Trading Strategies

Let's break it down with some of the most common algo trading strategies:

- **Trend Following:** Buy when prices are going up, sell when they're going down. Sounds simple, but there's an art to defining the trend.

- **Mean Reversion:** Assume prices will revert to a mean. Great when markets are choppy and range-bound. Terrible when markets break out and your algo insists it's just a blip.

- **Arbitrage:** Exploit tiny price differences between markets. Usually the domain of high-frequency trading, but some clever tricks exist for retail too.

- **Market Making:** Provide liquidity by constantly quoting buy and sell prices. It's like being the guy at the party always handing out drinks. Risky, but rewarding.

- **News-Based:** React to market-moving news, sometimes in milliseconds. You'll need data feeds faster than your cousin's crypto tips.
- **Machine Learning Models:** More advanced and complex, these can learn patterns from data. But be warned: garbage in, garbage out.

These are just broad categories. Within each, there's room for creativity, customization, and wild experimentation (responsibly, of course).

The Toolkit

You don't need to build your own Wall Street-grade infrastructure to get started. Here's what most algo traders use:

- **Programming Language:** Python is the go-to. R is popular in academia. C++ if you're brave and need blazing speed.
- **Broker API:** Interactive Brokers, Alpaca, and others offer APIs that let you place trades programmatically.
- **Backtesting Frameworks:** Tools like Backtrader, Zipline, or homemade scripts let you test strategies.
- **Data:** Historical, real-time, and sometimes alternative data (think social media sentiment, satellite imagery... yes, really).
- **Execution Logic:** Smart order routing, slippage control, and position sizing logic help you stay in the game.

Don't worry—we'll dig into all of this later. You'll go from "What's a pandas DataFrame?" to "I just built a regime-switching volatility model" faster than you think.

Final Thoughts (and One Last Joke)

So there you have it. Algorithmic trading is essentially using code to take your trading ideas and make them systematic, repeatable, and fast. It's powerful, scalable, and—if you do it right—profitable.

But remember, it's not magic. It's not plug-and-play riches. And if someone sells you an "AI-powered guaranteed 98% win rate bot" on Telegram... run. Probably barefoot. Preferably screaming.

I've seen algorithms succeed beyond expectations. I've also seen them crash and burn spectacularly, taking egos and savings accounts with them. The difference? Testing, risk management, and a healthy dose of humility.

And if you're still unsure whether algo trading is for you, just ask yourself: do I want to trust my emotions or trust my code? If your answer is "both," congratulations—you've just described 95% of my existential crises over the past 20 years.

Let's move on to the fun stuff. Now that you know what algorithmic trading is, let's dive into how to start crafting strategies that don't suck.

1.2 The Evolution of Trading Systems

When I started trading two decades ago, "cutting-edge technology" meant a squeaky chair, two monitors the size of microwaves, and a broker you could reach faster on the phone than through the internet. Now? Trading systems can execute a thousand trades before I finish typing the word "trade." The evolution has been nothing short of wild—like watching a house cat slowly morph into a tiger, then into a tiger with a jetpack.

Let's take a quick walk down memory lane (or in this case, the trading floor).

The Age of Shouting and Paper Slips

Long before code ruled the markets, traders ruled the floor. If you've ever seen old footage of stock exchanges—people yelling, waving papers, and making hand signals that look like a mix between charades and sign language—you've seen the open outcry system in action.

In those days, a "trading system" was essentially a human brain and a Rolodex of contacts. Decisions were made on the fly, often fueled by gut feelings, market gossip, and too much coffee. If someone says they "executed trades in seconds" back then, they probably meant thirty seconds, and only if the broker picked up the phone right away.

The Rise of Electronic Trading

Then came the first real disruption: electronic trading platforms in the 1980s and 1990s. Suddenly, the chaos of the pit started giving way to the quiet hum of computer terminals. These early systems were still basic compared to today's standards, but they were revolutionary.

Now, traders could enter orders directly into a computer without yelling at a guy across the room. Speed improved, execution costs dropped, and more people could access the markets without having to physically be on an exchange floor.

Of course, these systems were clunky. They were prone to crashes, had limited features, and looked about as user-friendly as a tax form. But they paved the way for what was to come.

The Birth of Retail Trading Platforms

By the late 1990s and early 2000s, online brokers and retail trading platforms exploded. Suddenly, anyone with a computer and an internet connection could trade from home. The barrier to entry dropped, and so did the excuses. The only real hurdle was your dial-up connection speed (and whether someone in your house picked up the phone mid-trade).

This democratization of trading was both exciting and dangerous. Exciting because it opened up opportunities for independent traders. Dangerous because it also opened the door for people with no experience to blow up accounts faster than you could say "margin call."

From Discretion to Systems

As access improved, so did the desire for systematic approaches. Traders started realizing that relying on emotion wasn't sustainable. Spreadsheets became the first "homebrew" trading systems—manually tracking indicators, backtesting strategies on historical data, and trying to find patterns.

But the real leap came when brokers began offering APIs, allowing traders to write scripts to automate parts (or all) of their process. No more manually clicking buy and sell buttons—the system could handle it based on predefined rules.

High-Frequency and Algorithmic Trading

The mid-2000s brought the rise of high-frequency trading (HFT). These were the Usain Bolts of the trading world—firms with advanced infrastructure capable of executing thousands of orders in microseconds. They used co-location (placing servers physically close to exchange servers) to shave off milliseconds, and their strategies relied on speed, precision, and scale.

While most retail traders can't (and shouldn't) compete with HFT, the technologies developed during this era—faster execution, smarter order routing, more data availability—filtered down to the broader market.

Algorithmic trading became not just a hedge fund game but something independent traders could explore. Cloud computing, machine learning, and open-source libraries made it accessible to people without deep pockets.

Today's Trading Systems

Fast-forward to today, and the landscape is mind-boggling:

- Fully automated systems capable of monitoring multiple markets in real-time
- Machine learning models analyzing terabytes of data for predictive signals
- Cloud-based platforms offering backtesting, live trading, and data streaming in one place
- Retail brokers providing commission-free trading and instant execution
- Integration of alternative data sources—satellite imagery, credit card transaction data, social media sentiment

And it's not slowing down. Advances in AI, quantum computing, and blockchain technology are already starting to seep into the world of trading systems.

The Human Element

With all this tech, you might think humans are obsolete in trading. Not quite. Systems still need ideas, oversight, and adaptation. Markets change. Strategies degrade. And no matter how smart your code is, it can't yet replicate the creativity (and occasional insanity) of human thinking.

In my own career, I've seen systems go from clunky desktop programs to sleek, cloud-based, API-driven powerhouses. But no matter the tech, the core principle hasn't changed: you're trying to find an edge and execute it consistently.

The Punchline

So, the evolution of trading systems is really a story of humans building tools to make themselves faster, smarter, and less emotional... only to spend the saved time arguing about which programming language is better. (For the record: Python. But I'll happily fight about it over coffee.)

From screaming across trading pits to coding in our pajamas, we've come a long way. And if history is any guide, the systems of tomorrow will make today's tech look like a stone tablet. Let's just hope they don't start sending us margin calls directly to our smart fridges.

1.3 Key Components of an Algorithmic Strategy

I've seen traders spend months building what they think is a "bulletproof" trading algorithm... only to realize they forgot one crucial thing: an actual exit plan. That's like building a spaceship and forgetting to add a way to land. Sure, you'll get off the ground, but the ending is going to be messy.

Over the years, I've learned that a solid algorithmic strategy isn't just some fancy math wrapped in code—it's a combination of key components that have to work together like a well-rehearsed band. If one player's off-key, the whole thing sounds terrible.

Let's break down the essential parts.

1. Market Selection

Before you write a single line of code, you need to decide what you're trading. Stocks? Futures? Forex? Crypto? Each market has its quirks—liquidity, volatility, trading hours, and transaction costs all vary.

For example, forex trades 24/5 and is heavily driven by macroeconomic events. Stocks have set trading hours and more regulatory constraints. Crypto never sleeps, which is exciting... and exhausting.

A good strategy starts with a clear choice of market and a deep understanding of how that market behaves. Otherwise, you're like someone designing a submarine without deciding whether it's for the ocean or your backyard pool.

2. Data

If market selection is the "where," data is the "what." You need quality historical and real-time data for your chosen market.

That means:

- **Historical data for backtesting** (price, volume, maybe even order book depth).
- **Real-time data for live trading** (low latency, reliable feeds).
- **Alternative data if you want an edge** (news sentiment, social media chatter, weather patterns—yes, some traders really track the weather).

Garbage data leads to garbage results. And I've seen traders spend weeks perfecting their logic only to discover their backtest was based on incorrect price feeds. It's like building a gourmet recipe with expired ingredients—don't expect a great meal.

3. Signal Generation

This is the brain of your strategy. Signals are the rules that decide when to buy, sell, or hold.

They can be based on:

- **Technical indicators** (moving averages, RSI, Bollinger Bands).
- **Price action** (breakouts, reversals, candlestick patterns).
- **Statistical methods** (mean reversion, correlation analysis).
- **Machine learning predictions** (if you want to get fancy).

Your signals need to be clear, testable, and unambiguous. If your rule is "buy when it looks bullish," congratulations—you've just automated indecision.

4. Risk Management

If signals are the brain, risk management is the immune system. It keeps your strategy alive when the market turns ugly.

Key elements include:

- **Position sizing:** Deciding how much to allocate per trade.
- **Stop-loss levels:** Capping your downside.
- **Take-profit targets:** Locking in gains before the market changes its mind.
- **Max drawdown limits:** Pausing or shutting down the system when losses exceed a threshold.

I can't stress this enough—risk management is not optional. Without it, you're just a gambler with a faster computer.

5. Execution Logic

It's one thing to have a signal—it's another to get that trade into the market efficiently.

Execution logic covers how your orders are placed:

- Market vs. limit orders.
- Order splitting to avoid moving the market.
- Slippage control (because the price you want and the price you get can be different).
- Smart order routing (for multi-exchange strategies).

A brilliant strategy can still lose money if it executes poorly. Think of it like a race car with a world-class driver but four flat tires.

6. Backtesting and Optimization

This is where you take your historical data and see how your strategy would have performed in the past.

But here's the trap: overfitting. If you tweak your strategy until it performs perfectly on historical data, you might just be tailoring it to past noise, not future opportunities. It's like studying last year's test answers and expecting the exact same questions again.

Good backtesting uses:

- **Out-of-sample data** (data your system hasn't "seen" before).
- **Walk-forward testing** (rolling tests to simulate changing markets).
- **Sensitivity analysis** (seeing how small changes in parameters affect results).

7. Monitoring and Maintenance

Even after your strategy goes live, the work isn't over. Markets change. Infrastructure breaks. Data feeds drop.

Monitoring involves:

- Tracking performance in real-time.
- Watching for unusual patterns or execution issues.
- Making adjustments when market conditions shift.

A "set and forget" algorithm is a myth. You might not have to watch it every second, but ignoring it completely is asking for trouble.

The Wrap-Up

A good algorithmic strategy is like a recipe—each ingredient matters, and skipping one can ruin the dish. Market selection, data, signal generation, risk management, execution, backtesting, and ongoing monitoring—they all have to work together.

Ignore any of these, and you're basically walking into a boxing match with one glove. Sure, you might land a punch, but don't be surprised if the market knocks you out first.

And remember: the strategy you start with probably won't be the one you stick with forever. In my experience, it's a constant process of testing, refining, and occasionally deleting the whole thing and starting fresh... preferably without swearing too loudly at your laptop.

1.4 Manual vs. Automated Trading

I still remember my early days of manual trading—sitting at my desk with three coffee cups, two charts, and one heart rate monitor that was basically there for entertainment. Manual trading felt like being the pilot of a fighter jet: thrilling, stressful, and one bad decision away from disaster.

Fast forward a couple of decades, and I'm mostly running automated systems that don't get nervous when the market spikes. The difference between manual and automated trading isn't just about speed—it's about mindset, consistency, and how much you enjoy staring at screens until your eyes water.

What Is Manual Trading?

Manual trading is exactly what it sounds like: you make the trading decisions and place the orders yourself. It's the oldest style of trading, and for many, still the most intuitive.

Typical process:

- You watch the market in real-time.
- You identify an opportunity based on your analysis.
- You manually enter an order through your broker's platform.
- You manage and close the position yourself.

It's active, it's personal, and it gives you total control. The flip side? It also leaves you at the mercy of your emotions, distractions, and reaction time.

What Is Automated Trading?

Automated trading replaces (or assists) the human decision-making process with pre-defined rules executed by a computer program. The system monitors markets, generates signals, and places orders—sometimes in milliseconds—without you lifting a finger.

You can automate:

- **Signal generation** (when to buy or sell)
- **Order execution** (how to place trades)
- **Risk management** (stop-losses, position sizing)
- **Monitoring and alerts**

The biggest difference is that in automated trading, you do the thinking before the trade happens. You code your logic, test it, and let it run.

Key Differences

1. Speed

Manual: Limited by human reaction time—seconds at best.

Automated: Executes in milliseconds. In fast-moving markets, that can mean the difference between a win and a loss.

2. Consistency

Manual: Performance can vary depending on mood, fatigue, or whether you've had your morning coffee.

Automated: Same rules, same execution, every time.

3. Complexity

Manual: Easier to start, harder to scale.

Automated: More upfront work (coding, testing), but easier to scale across multiple markets and assets.

4. Flexibility

Manual: You can adapt instantly to unexpected market events.

Automated: Adapts only if you've coded it to handle those scenarios.

5. Emotional Control

Manual: Prone to fear, greed, and panic.

Automated: Zero emotions—unless you count your reaction when it makes or loses money.

When Manual Trading Makes Sense

- **Learning the basics:** Manual trading teaches market structure, order types, and discipline.
- **Low-frequency strategies:** If you trade once or twice a week, automation might be overkill.
- **Complex judgment calls:** Certain trades require human interpretation of nuanced news or events.

When Automated Trading Shines

- **High-frequency strategies:** Too fast for human hands.
- **Multiple markets:** One person can't realistically monitor 50 charts at once, but a program can.
- **Rule-based strategies:** When your logic is clear and testable, automation can execute flawlessly.

The Hybrid Approach

Some traders blend the two—running automated systems for scanning and alerts, but pulling the trigger manually. Others use automation for execution but still decide the direction themselves.

This hybrid method can be a good bridge for traders transitioning from manual to fully automated trading. It keeps you engaged without relying entirely on your caffeine-powered reflexes.

The Trade-Off

Here's the truth: neither manual nor automated trading is "better" in all situations. They're tools. Manual trading gives flexibility and intuition; automated trading gives speed and consistency.

Over my career, I've moved from 100% manual to 90% automated. I still do the occasional manual trade—usually when I see something my algos aren't built to catch—but I prefer letting the machines take the emotional rollercoaster for me.

Final Thought

Think of manual trading like cooking dinner yourself: you get total control, you can improvise, and sometimes it's deeply satisfying. Automated trading is like having a skilled chef who follows your recipe perfectly, every time, while you sit on the couch.

The key is deciding when you want to be in the kitchen, and when you'd rather let the chef work. Just don't forget—whether you or the chef makes it—if the recipe's bad, the meal will still taste terrible.

1.5 The Role of Technology in Modern Markets

If you dropped a trader from the 1980s into today's markets, they'd probably think they'd walked into a sci-fi movie. Back then, "high tech" meant a pager, a fax machine, and maybe—if you were really fancy—a Bloomberg terminal that looked like it could survive a small explosion. Now? We've got trading systems running in the cloud, AI models analyzing terabytes of data, and retail traders placing orders from their phones while standing in line for coffee.

Technology hasn't just changed the markets—it's completely rewritten the rules of engagement.

Speed: The New Currency

In modern markets, milliseconds matter. High-frequency trading firms literally spend millions shaving microseconds off their order times—moving servers closer to exchange data centers, optimizing network cables, and using microwave transmission lines instead of fiber for faster data transfer.

For retail traders, you don't need to be in the microsecond game, but you do benefit from this infrastructure. Order execution is faster, slippage is lower, and you can see market data almost instantly. The gap between professional and individual traders has shrunk—not closed entirely, but a lot smaller than it used to be.

Data: The Lifeblood of Trading

We're drowning in data. Price, volume, order book depth, news headlines, social media sentiment, economic releases, even satellite images of store parking lots.

Modern technology has turned data collection and processing into a science. You can:

- Stream real-time prices to your laptop or phone.
- Backtest strategies using decades of historical data.
- Incorporate alternative datasets for unique insights.

In my early days, getting historical tick-by-tick data meant begging your broker or paying a small fortune. Now, you can download it in minutes—or sometimes even free. The challenge isn't getting data anymore; it's knowing which data actually matters.

Automation and Algorithms

Trading systems today can scan thousands of instruments, generate signals, and execute orders—all without human intervention. This means:

- You can run multiple strategies at once.
- The system never sleeps or misses an opportunity.
- Emotions are removed from execution.

And with advances in programming frameworks, you don't need to be a software engineer to get started. Python, open APIs, and cloud computing have lowered the barrier to entry dramatically.

The Cloud and Remote Trading

Remember when trading meant sitting at a desk, glued to multiple monitors? Now you can manage trades from anywhere. Cloud-based platforms allow you to:

- Host your trading algorithms on remote servers for 24/7 operation.
- Access your account securely from any device.
- Scale up without investing in physical infrastructure.

I've literally monitored positions from a beach chair before—though I wouldn't call that a "best practice." Sand and laptops don't mix.

Machine Learning and AI

Artificial intelligence isn't just a buzzword—it's making a real impact in trading. Machine learning models can identify patterns too complex for traditional statistical methods, adapt to changing market conditions, and even process unstructured data like text or images.

Of course, AI isn't a magic bullet. You still need good data, sensible model design, and a healthy respect for the fact that markets can surprise you. But in the right hands, AI is a powerful addition to the trader's toolkit.

Connectivity and Global Access

Technology has flattened the world of trading. You can trade US stocks from Singapore, forex from London, or crypto from anywhere with an internet connection.

Global markets are now interconnected, meaning events in one corner of the world can ripple through others in seconds. A central bank announcement in Japan can move the S&P 500 futures in Chicago almost instantly. This interconnectedness creates both opportunity and risk—and technology is the bridge that makes it possible.

Risks of Technology Dependence

It's not all sunshine and perfect fills. Technology brings its own set of risks:

- **System failures:** Servers crash, code breaks, data feeds drop.
- **Cybersecurity threats:** Hacks and phishing can compromise accounts.
- **Over-automation:** Relying entirely on machines can lead to big losses if your logic is flawed.

I've had systems freeze mid-trade and algorithms go rogue due to a single typo. (Yes, one misplaced decimal point can ruin your day.)

The Balance

In today's markets, technology is a necessity. It's what allows traders—both retail and institutional—to compete, adapt, and innovate. But it's also a tool, not a replacement for judgment. The most successful traders I know combine the speed and efficiency of modern tech with human oversight, strategic thinking, and the ability to pull the plug when something looks wrong.

Closing Thought

Technology in modern markets is like electricity: invisible when it's working, chaos when it's not. It's made trading faster, smarter, and more accessible than ever before. But it's also made the game more complex, competitive, and unforgiving.

The trick is to let the machines do the heavy lifting while you keep your hands on the steering wheel. Otherwise, you might find yourself explaining to your broker why your "brilliant" AI bought 5,000 shares of the wrong stock at 3 a.m. on a Sunday.

Chapter 2: Market Microstructure and Data

Think of the market as a wild jungle safari. You've got predators (market makers), prey (retail investors), and some surprisingly sneaky creatures called HFTs darting through the underbrush. To survive here, you need to know who's who, what kind of data they're watching, and how orders really get filled when you hit that shiny green button.

In this chapter, we delve into the structure of modern financial markets by examining the participants, order types, and execution mechanisms. We break down the bid-ask spread, define liquidity, and differentiate between various levels of market data. Additionally, the chapter addresses the impact of latency and slippage—key considerations for algorithmic traders aiming for efficient execution.

2.1 Understanding Market Participants

When people first start trading, they tend to think the "market" is some single, mysterious entity—like a giant brain in the sky that decides prices just to mess with them personally. I hate to break it to you, but the market isn't out to get you. It's just a giant crowd of very different players, each with their own motives, timeframes, and—let's be honest—quirks.

If you want to trade successfully, you need to know who you're up against, who you're working alongside, and who you might accidentally be feeding profits to.

The Main Categories

Let's look at the biggest groups in the modern market arena.

1. Retail Traders (a.k.a. People Like Us)

Retail traders are individual investors—folks trading from home, their office, or occasionally a suspiciously quiet corner of the coffee shop. They might be day traders, swing traders, or long-term investors managing personal portfolios.

Strengths:

- Flexibility—no board of directors to answer to.
- Ability to move in and out of positions without impacting price much.

Weaknesses:

- Often undercapitalized compared to institutions.
- Prone to emotional decisions.
- Limited access to top-tier data and execution speed.

I've been in this camp for most of my career, and let me tell you—being small can be an advantage if you know how to stay nimble. But it also means you can't muscle the market around. You play with the flow, not against it.

2. Institutional Investors

This group includes mutual funds, pension funds, and insurance companies. They move big money—sometimes billions—and their trades can move markets.

Strengths:

- Huge capital reserves.
- Access to research, data, and connections retail traders can only dream of.

Weaknesses:

- Slow to act due to bureaucratic decision-making.
- Can't always exit positions without impacting price.

Institutions are like ocean liners—steady, powerful, but slow to turn. If you can spot what they're doing early, you can often ride the wake.

3. Hedge Funds

Hedge funds are the high-octane sports cars of the market world. They can be aggressive, secretive, and incredibly creative with their strategies—ranging from long/short equity to global macro to complex derivatives.

Strengths:

- **Flexible mandate**—can trade almost anything.
- Willingness to take calculated risks.

Weaknesses:

- High pressure to perform.
- Strategies can fail spectacularly.

Some hedge funds use algorithmic trading at massive scale, competing directly with other quant funds. If you're building algos, these guys might be your unseen competition.

4. High-Frequency Traders (HFTs)

These are the speed demons. HFT firms use ultra-fast algorithms to capitalize on microsecond opportunities—tiny inefficiencies in price that disappear almost instantly.

Strengths:

- Speed beyond human reaction.
- Huge trade volumes.

Weaknesses:

- Strategies are highly sensitive to market structure changes.
- Massive infrastructure costs.

You can't compete with them on speed. Don't even try. Instead, focus on areas where their edge is irrelevant.

5. Market Makers

Market makers provide liquidity by constantly quoting both buy and sell prices. Their job is to make sure there's always someone to take the other side of a trade.

Strengths:

- Profit from bid-ask spreads.
- Influence on market liquidity.

Weaknesses:

- Need to manage risk from holding inventory.

They're like the bartenders of the market—always there to serve, but not necessarily rooting for you.

6. Governments and Central Banks

Yes, they're in the market too—especially in forex and bonds. Central banks intervene to stabilize currencies, control inflation, and support economic policy.

Strengths:

- Unlimited capital (they can print it).
- Ability to move entire markets with a single statement.

Weaknesses:

- Bound by political objectives.

You can't fight a central bank. If they're buying or selling, the market listens.

7. Corporate Players

Corporations buy and sell their own shares (buybacks) or hedge currency and commodity exposures. Mergers, acquisitions, and earnings reports can create big moves.

Strengths:

- Insider knowledge of their own business.

Weaknesses:

- Limited to their own stock or market segment.

Why It Matters for You

Knowing the different market participants helps you:

- Understand price movements (big institutions leave footprints).
- Avoid competing directly with traders who have unfair advantages.
- Identify where your niche or edge might be.

If you're a retail algo trader, for example, your edge might come from exploiting inefficiencies that institutions overlook, or trading markets where HFT isn't dominant.

Final Thought

The market is like a giant multiplayer game—some players have better gear, some have more experience, and some are just there for the thrill. Your job isn't to beat everyone; it's to know who's in the game, what they're trying to do, and how you can carve out your own profitable space without getting steamrolled.

And if you ever start to feel paranoid that the "market" is targeting you personally... well, relax. It's not personal. You're just a small fish in a very big pond. Unless, of course, you're suddenly trading against a central bank. In that case—yes, it's probably personal.

2.2 Order Types and Execution Mechanics

One of the fastest ways I've seen new traders lose money is by clicking the wrong order type. I'm not exaggerating—place a "market buy" when you meant "limit sell," and you can go from confident to confused in about half a second. Trust me, I've been there.

Before you let an algorithm loose in the market, you have to understand how orders actually get from your screen (or your code) to the exchange, and how the market decides whether your trade gets filled, partially filled, or ignored entirely.

The Core Order Types

1. Market Order

A market order says, "Buy or sell this thing right now at the best available price." It's the simplest and fastest type of order, but also the riskiest if the market is moving quickly or has thin liquidity.

Pros:

- Immediate execution.
- Easy to use.

Cons:

- No control over price.
- Vulnerable to slippage.

I think of market orders like ordering food without looking at the price—you'll get fed, but you might regret it when the bill arrives.

2. Limit Order

A limit order says, "Buy at this price or better" (or "Sell at this price or better"). You're setting your terms, and the market either meets them or doesn't.

Pros:

- Price control.
- Can be used strategically to enter or exit at exact levels.

Cons:

- No guarantee of execution.
- In fast markets, you might get left behind.

I've had limit orders just sit there like a wallflower at a school dance—waiting for someone to come over, only to be ignored all night.

3. Stop Order (Stop-Loss or Stop-Buy)

A stop order becomes a market order once the stop price is hit. Used for protecting profits or limiting losses, and for entering trades when price breaks a certain level.

Pros:

- Automates risk management.
- Can help catch breakouts.

Cons:

- Once triggered, you're subject to market order slippage.

Stops are like fire alarms—you hope they never go off, but you'll be glad they do when the kitchen starts smoking.

4. Stop-Limit Order

This is a combination of a stop and a limit. Once your stop is hit, a limit order is placed instead of a market order.

Pros:

- Control over price after trigger.

Cons:

- You might not get filled if the market moves quickly past your limit.

It's the "I'll evacuate, but only if the bus fare is right" version of a stop order.

5. Other Order Types

Depending on your broker and market, you might also see:

- **Trailing Stops:** Adjusts automatically as the market moves in your favor.

- **Fill or Kill (FOK):** Must be executed immediately in full or not at all.

- **Immediate or Cancel (IOC):** Fill whatever can be filled right now, cancel the rest.

- **Good 'Til Cancelled (GTC):** Stays active until you cancel it.

Order Execution Mechanics

The Journey of an Order

When you place an order, it travels from your trading platform to your broker's system, then to the exchange (or multiple exchanges). Along the way, your broker's routing logic decides where to send it for the best possible fill.

In some markets, your order may hit an order book—a list of all buy and sell orders currently resting at each price level. Matching occurs when a buy order meets a sell order at the same price.

Market Depth and Liquidity

Execution quality depends on liquidity—how many buyers and sellers there are at each price.

- In highly liquid markets, your orders fill quickly and with minimal slippage.
- In thin markets, large orders can move the price against you.

Slippage and Partial Fills

- **Slippage:** The difference between your expected price and the actual fill price.
- **Partial Fill:** Only part of your order gets executed because there weren't enough shares/contracts available at your price.

Slippage is inevitable sometimes, but good execution logic can minimize it. Partial fills... well, they're just part of trading life.

Smart Order Routing

Brokers and trading algorithms often use smart order routing to split large orders across multiple venues to get better prices or more liquidity. This is especially important in fragmented markets (like US equities) where trading happens across multiple exchanges.

Why This Matters in Algorithmic Trading

When coding a strategy, your "paper trading" fills are often perfect. In reality, orders face latency, liquidity constraints, and routing decisions. That's why live performance can differ from backtests.

If your algo assumes instant fills at exact prices, it's living in a fantasy world. You need to model slippage, delays, and partial fills in testing to avoid nasty surprises.

Final Thought

Order types are your basic vocabulary in the market, and execution mechanics are the grammar rules. Get them wrong, and you might be saying something very different than you intended—like telling your broker to buy into a crash instead of selling out of it.

So before you unleash your algorithm, make sure it speaks fluent "order execution." Otherwise, you might find yourself watching in horror as your perfectly good idea gets mangled somewhere between your keyboard and the exchange.

2.3 Bid-Ask Spread and Liquidity

When I first heard the term "bid-ask spread," I thought it sounded like some kind of exotic trading strategy or a fancy Wall Street lunch special. Spoiler: it's neither. It's actually one of the most basic, yet most important, concepts in market mechanics. And if you don't understand it, the market will happily tax your ignorance, one trade at a time.

The Basics

In any market, there are two prices at any given moment:

- **Bid:** The highest price someone is willing to pay to buy.
- **Ask (or "offer"):** The lowest price someone is willing to accept to sell.

The bid-ask spread is the difference between these two numbers.

Example:

- **Bid:** $100.00
- **Ask:** $100.05
- **Spread:** $0.05

That spread is the cost of doing business. Every time you cross it—by buying at the ask or selling at the bid—you're paying someone for liquidity.

Who Makes the Spread?

Market makers, high-frequency traders, and other liquidity providers profit from the spread. They buy at the bid, sell at the ask, and pocket the difference (minus costs). This role is crucial because it keeps the market functioning smoothly—without them, you might struggle to find someone to take the other side of your trade.

Tight vs. Wide Spreads

- **Tight Spread:** Often found in highly liquid markets like major forex pairs or large-cap stocks. This means low transaction costs and usually better fills.

- **Wide Spread:** Common in illiquid assets, penny stocks, or during volatile market conditions. This increases costs and makes execution trickier.

I've seen traders jump into a low-liquidity stock with a $0.50 spread, thinking they'd found a bargain. In reality, they paid a premium just to get in—and then another to get out.

Liquidity: The Other Half of the Story

Liquidity measures how easily you can enter or exit a position without moving the price too much. It's influenced by:

- **Number of participants:** More buyers and sellers = more liquidity.

- **Order book depth:** How many orders are resting at each price level.

- **Market activity:** Busy markets (like during major sessions) are more liquid.

High Liquidity Markets

- Narrow spreads

- Faster execution

- Less slippage

Low Liquidity Markets

- Wide spreads
- Risk of partial fills
- Higher price impact from large orders

Why It Matters for Algorithmic Trading

If you're running a high-frequency or scalping strategy, spreads can make or break you. A strategy that looks profitable in backtesting might turn negative once real spreads are factored in.

For swing or position trading, liquidity still matters—illiquid markets can trap you in trades you'd rather exit. I've personally had a "get me out now" moment turn into "get me out next week" because there simply weren't enough buyers at my price.

Spread Behavior

Spreads aren't static. They can widen during:

- Low-volume periods (like after hours).
- Economic announcements.
- Sudden volatility spikes.

Automated systems should be designed to detect and adapt to spread changes—sometimes it's better to pause trading when spreads blow out.

The Takeaway

Bid-ask spread and liquidity are the invisible tollbooths of trading. You pay them every time you cross the road between buying and selling. Understanding how they work—and how they vary across markets and conditions—can save you a lot of small but consistent losses that quietly eat into profits.

And remember, in trading as in life, sometimes the difference between a smooth ride and a bumpy one comes down to knowing when not to take the expensive shortcut. Or in this case, the wide spread.

2.4 Market Data Types: Level I vs Level II

When I first signed up for a live trading platform, I remember feeling slightly cheated. I thought I'd see a magical Wall Street dashboard with blinking lights, streaming numbers, and maybe someone shouting "Buy!" into a phone. Instead, I got a clean chart and a tiny window showing the bid and ask. That was my introduction to Level I market data.

It wasn't until later—after a few unnecessarily expensive mistakes—that I discovered Level II data and realized, "Oh... so this is what the pros are watching."

Level I Market Data

Level I is the bread-and-butter feed for most traders. It's what you typically get by default when you open a brokerage account. It includes:

- **Best Bid:** The highest price someone's willing to buy at right now.
- **Best Ask:** The lowest price someone's willing to sell at right now.
- **Last Price:** The price of the most recent trade.
- **Volume:** How many shares/contracts have traded in the session.

Level I gives you a snapshot of the market at its most accessible point. You can make trading decisions with just this data—plenty of retail traders do—but it's a bit like knowing the weather in one neighborhood when you're trying to plan a road trip.

Level II Market Data

Level II goes deeper. It shows the order book—the list of buy and sell orders at various price levels beyond just the best bid and ask. You'll see:

- **Multiple Bid Levels:** All the buy orders stacked below the current best bid.

- **Multiple Ask Levels:** All the sell orders stacked above the current best ask.

- **Order Sizes:** How many shares/contracts are sitting at each price.

- **Market Participants:** In some feeds, you can see which firms or market makers are posting those orders.

With Level II, you're essentially getting an x-ray of market liquidity. You can spot where big players might be sitting, waiting to absorb or push through orders.

How Traders Use Them

With Level I Data:

- Scalpers and day traders use it for quick in-and-out trades.

- Swing traders rely on it for basic execution decisions.

- Algorithms use it for simple signal generation and price triggers.

With Level II Data:

- You can anticipate short-term support/resistance by seeing where large order clusters sit.

- You can detect potential spoofing or sudden liquidity changes.

- High-frequency traders use it to predict micro-price movements.

Limitations and Gotchas

- **Level I:** Doesn't show depth. If you see a tight spread, it might be hiding the fact that the rest of the order book is thin.

- **Level II:** More information doesn't always mean better decisions. Order books can be deceptive—some orders are pulled before they execute, and large hidden orders ("icebergs") won't show at all.

In Algorithmic Trading

Level I data is often enough for longer-term strategies, but if your algorithm needs to react to microstructure changes—like detecting when liquidity disappears before a big move—Level II can give you the edge.

That said, processing Level II data requires more bandwidth, more complex coding, and careful filtering to avoid drowning in noise.

The Bottom Line

Think of Level I as reading the headlines, and Level II as reading the full article, including the footnotes. The first will keep you informed, the second can give you deeper insight—but only if you know how to interpret it.

And remember: just because you can see ten layers deep into the market doesn't mean you suddenly have Jedi powers. Sometimes you're just seeing more people in line to get trampled when the stampede starts.

2.5 Latency and Slippage Considerations

When I first started automating trades, I assumed the market would politely wait for my orders to arrive. Spoiler: it didn't. By the time my "perfect" buy signal fired, the price had already run off like a toddler in a toy store. That's when I learned two of the least glamorous but most important words in algorithmic trading: latency and slippage.

What Is Latency?

Latency is the delay between when your trading system sends an order and when that order is actually received and acted upon by the exchange.

It can happen at multiple points:

1. **Signal Processing Delay** – Your code takes time to crunch numbers and decide to trade.
2. **Transmission Delay** – Sending the order from your machine to your broker's server.
3. **Broker Processing Delay** – Broker systems queue, check, and route orders.
4. **Exchange Matching Delay** – The time it takes the exchange to match your order with a counterparty.

Why It Matters

- In fast-moving markets, even milliseconds matter.

- Latency can mean the difference between buying low and buying slightly-higher-than-you-wanted.

- High-frequency traders spend fortunes shaving microseconds off latency—think co-location servers parked right next to exchange infrastructure.

For most retail traders, we don't need to go full "NASA mission control" mode, but we still need to be aware of how delays impact fills.

What Is Slippage?

Slippage is the difference between the price you expected to get and the price you actually got when your order executed.

Example:

- You send a market order expecting $50.00.
- The order fills at $50.04.
- That $0.04 difference is slippage.

Causes of Slippage

- **Low Liquidity:** Not enough volume at your desired price.
- **High Volatility:** Prices moving quickly between order submission and execution.
- **Latency:** Orders getting filled after the market moves.
- **Large Order Size:** Your trade eats through available orders at the best price and spills into worse prices.

The Relationship Between Latency and Slippage

Think of latency as the time gap and slippage as the cost of that gap. If your order arrives late in a fast-moving market, the price might be gone, and you pay more (or receive less) than planned.

Managing Latency

- **Optimize Code:** Minimize unnecessary calculations in your trading logic.

- **Efficient Data Handling:** Don't process more data than you need.

- **Proximity to Broker:** Using a VPS close to your broker's servers can cut network delays.

- **Right Infrastructure:** If serious about speed, look into co-location (though it's pricey).

Managing Slippage

- **Use Limit Orders:** Control the worst price you'll accept.

- **Avoid Thin Markets:** Trade in instruments with good liquidity.

- **Reduce Trade Size:** Avoid moving the market with your order.

- **Time Your Trades:** Avoid high-volatility announcements unless that's part of your strategy.

- **Model Slippage in Backtests:** Add realistic assumptions so your performance estimates aren't fantasyland numbers.

In Algorithmic Trading

An algo might look fantastic in a backtest with perfect fills, but real-world latency and slippage can turn those projected profits into disappointment. That's why serious strategy development includes execution simulation—factoring in time delays and realistic fill prices.

The Takeaway

Latency and slippage aren't glamorous, but they're like gravity—you don't notice them until they're pulling you down. Understanding them, measuring them, and building systems that minimize them is what separates hobby projects from real, money-making trading algorithms.

And remember: the market isn't going to wait for you to catch up. If your algo's too slow, it's like showing up to a flash sale after the doors close—you'll still get inside, but all the good deals will be gone.

Chapter 3: Programming for Traders

If you've ever shouted at your screen, "WHY DID YOU BUY THAT?!"—good news, your future trading bot won't take offense. But first, you'll have to teach it how to think (and not blow up your account). Time to choose your digital weapon of choice—Python, C++, or that Excel sheet you've been duct-taping for years.

This chapter focuses on equipping traders with the technical tools needed for algorithm development. Topics include choosing an appropriate programming language, setting up a development environment, working with essential libraries, integrating with broker APIs, and coding a simple trading strategy to lay the foundation for more complex systems.

3.1 Choosing a Programming Language (Python, C++, etc.)

When I first decided to code my own trading strategies, I thought the hardest part would be coming up with profitable ideas. Nope. The hardest part was staring at a list of programming languages and trying to pick one without feeling like I was choosing a tattoo I'd regret later.

Ask ten algo traders which language is best, and you'll get twelve different answers—plus a heated debate that could outlast a congressional hearing.

Why Language Choice Matters

The programming language you choose determines:

- Speed of execution
- Ease of development
- Available libraries and frameworks
- Community support
- Integration with brokers and data providers

For some traders, language choice is like religion—once they've chosen, they're committed for life. For others, it's purely practical: whatever gets the job done fastest (and cheapest) wins.

Python: The Swiss Army Knife

If algorithmic trading had a "most popular" award, Python would win by a landslide.

Pros:

- Easy to learn and read—great for beginners.

- Massive ecosystem of trading, data science, and machine learning libraries (Pandas, NumPy, scikit-learn, TA-Lib, backtrader).
- Integrates well with APIs and data feeds.
- Huge community—answers to most problems are a Google search away.

Cons:

- Slower than compiled languages (like C++).
- Performance can be an issue for ultra-low-latency strategies.

Best For: Rapid prototyping, research, and most retail trading strategies.

C++: The Speed Demon

C++ is the choice for traders who measure time in microseconds and consider "latency" a personal insult.

Pros:

- Blazing-fast execution.
- Fine control over memory and processing.
- Preferred in institutional high-frequency trading (HFT).

Cons:

- Steeper learning curve.
- Development time is longer compared to Python.
- Debugging can be more painful.

Best For: HFT, ultra-low-latency execution, and situations where every nanosecond matters.

Java: The Middle Ground

Java sits between Python's ease and C++'s speed.

Pros:

- Faster than Python in many cases.
- Cross-platform compatibility.
- Good for multi-threaded applications.

Cons:

- Verbose code—takes more lines to do the same thing.
- Not as many specialized trading libraries as Python.

Best For: Multi-asset, event-driven systems that need decent speed and stability.

Other Languages Worth Mentioning

- **C#:** Popular for traders using platforms like NinjaTrader. Good performance, strong Microsoft ecosystem.
- **R:** Excellent for statistical modeling and research, but not ideal for live execution.
- **MATLAB:** Great for quantitative research and prototyping—expensive license.
- **Julia:** Newer, designed for high-performance numerical computing.

How to Choose

Ask yourself:

- **What's my latency requirement?** If you're not competing in microseconds, Python will probably do.

- **What's my current skill level?** If you're new to coding, Python's learning curve is much kinder.

- **What's my goal?** Rapid prototyping or production-grade HFT system?

- **Who will maintain it?** If it's just you, choose a language you enjoy working in.

My Personal Take

I use Python for 90% of my work—it's fast enough for my strategies, easy to maintain, and the library support is unbeatable. When I need something lightning-fast, I offload the heavy-lifting parts to C++ modules and keep Python as the "glue" that holds the system together.

It's like using a sports car for most trips but keeping a Formula 1 car in the garage for the rare race day.

The Bottom Line

The "best" programming language is the one that balances performance, development speed, and your skill set. Don't get paralyzed by choice—start with the language that lets you build something now, and optimize later if needed.

And remember: nobody ever lost money because their code was written in the wrong language—they lost money because their code told them to buy at the top.

3.2 Essential Libraries and Tools

When I first sat down to code my first trading bot, I imagined myself like some kind of financial Tony Stark—screens glowing, charts flickering, algorithms humming. In reality, I spent the first two days just trying to install the right Python libraries without breaking my laptop. Lesson learned: the tools you choose can make or break your sanity before you've even placed your first trade.

Why Tools Matter

In algorithmic trading, your tools are the difference between spending your time building strategies and spending your time Googling why your script can't find "numpy." The right libraries and platforms help you:

- Process market data quickly
- Test strategies accurately
- Connect to brokers and exchanges
- Monitor live trades without babysitting your screen 24/7

Python Libraries You'll Use Constantly

1. Pandas – Your bread and butter for working with time series data. Think of it as Excel on steroids, but without the "why did my cell just turn into a date?" headaches.

2. NumPy – For fast numerical computations. When Pandas needs raw speed, it secretly calls NumPy behind the scenes.

3. TA-Lib – A huge library of technical analysis indicators (moving averages, RSI, MACD, Bollinger Bands—you name it).

4. **Matplotlib / Plotly** – For visualizing your strategies, backtests, and performance metrics. Matplotlib is the classic, Plotly is the flashy one with interactive charts.

5. **scikit-learn** – Machine learning for things like classification, regression, and clustering—handy if you want your strategy to adapt and learn.

6. **backtrader** – A great framework for backtesting and running live strategies without reinventing the wheel.

7. **yfinance** – For pulling historical market data directly from Yahoo Finance (great for prototyping).

Tools for Development

- **Jupyter Notebook** – Lets you write, run, and document code interactively. Perfect for experimenting and testing ideas.

- **VS Code** – Lightweight, fast, and has tons of extensions for Python, C++, Git integration, and debugging.

- **PyCharm** – More heavyweight but excellent for big projects with lots of files.

- **Git & GitHub/GitLab** – Version control is your safety net. Without it, you're one "accidental save" away from erasing three months of work.

Data Access Tools

- **CCXT** – A unified API for dozens of crypto exchanges. Saves you from learning each one's quirks.

- **IBKR API (Interactive Brokers)** – If you're into stocks, options, futures, and forex, IBKR's API is the Swiss Army knife.

- **Alpaca API** – Commission-free trading for US stocks with a Python-friendly API.

- **Polygon.io / Quandl** – Paid data sources with robust APIs and more reliable coverage than most free feeds.

Infrastructure Helpers

- **Docker** – Lets you run your trading bot in a clean, consistent environment no matter where you deploy it.
- **Celery / Airflow** – For scheduling and managing complex workflows (like fetching data, processing it, and executing trades at specific times).
- **Redis** – In-memory database for lightning-fast temporary storage (great for caching market data).

My Recommended Starter Kit

If I were starting from scratch today, here's what I'd install on day one for Python-based algo trading:

- **VS Code** (editor)
- **Git + GitHub** (version control)
- **Python 3.11** (latest stable release)
- **Pandas, NumPy,** TA-Lib, Matplotlib, backtrader, yfinance (core libraries)
- **Jupyter Notebook** (idea testing)

That's enough to start prototyping strategies, backtesting them, and even running some basic live trades.

The Upgrade Path

As your strategies get more advanced, you might add:

- scikit-learn or TensorFlow/PyTorch for machine learning.

- Plotly Dash for creating a live dashboard of your trading bot.
- PostgreSQL or MongoDB for long-term data storage.
- Docker + Cloud Hosting (AWS, Azure, GCP) to keep your bot running 24/7.

The Bottom Line

Don't get lost in "tool collecting." I've met traders who spend months setting up the perfect tech stack and never actually run a trade. Pick the essentials, get your system working, then add more tools as you outgrow your setup.

And remember: the fanciest library in the world won't save you from a bad strategy—just like the best chef's knife won't make instant noodles taste like a five-star meal.

3.3 Setting Up Your Development Environment

When I first started algorithmic trading, I thought "development environment" meant clearing enough desk space for my laptop and coffee. Turns out, it's less about desk clutter and more about getting your software, libraries, and tools to all play nicely together—without turning your computer into a very expensive paperweight.

Why Your Environment Matters

A stable, well-organized development environment is like a clean kitchen for a chef. If you have your knives, pans, and spices where you need them, you can cook without running to the store mid-recipe. In trading terms, it means:

- Faster setup for new projects
- Less "it works on my machine" problems
- Smooth testing and deployment
- Easier debugging when something breaks (and something will break)

Step 1: Install Python (or Your Chosen Language)

If you're going the Python route—and most traders do—download the latest stable release from python.org or use Anaconda if you want a pre-packaged environment with most libraries preinstalled.

Pro tip: Avoid using the Python version that comes with your operating system—it's usually outdated and can cause compatibility nightmares.

Step 2: Use Virtual Environments

A virtual environment keeps each project's dependencies separate so that one project's upgrade doesn't wreck another.

For Python:

 # Install virtualenv

pip install virtualenv

 # Create a new environment

virtualenv my_trading_env

 # Activate it (Windows)

my_trading_env\Scripts\activate

 # Activate it (Mac/Linux)

source my_trading_env/bin/activate

Think of it as giving each of your bots their own little sandbox so they don't throw sand in each other's eyes.

Step 3: Pick Your IDE

- **Your IDE** (Integrated Development Environment) is your cockpit. My top picks:
- **VS Code** – Lightweight, customizable, lots of extensions.
- **PyCharm** – Heavier, but packed with advanced features for larger projects.
- **Jupyter Notebook** – Great for prototyping and visualizing data before moving to production code.

Set up syntax highlighting, linting (like Pylint), and code formatting (like Black) to keep your code readable and consistent.

Step 4: Install Core Libraries

Before you start coding, load up your virtual environment with the essentials:

pip install pandas numpy matplotlib backtrader yfinance TA-Lib

This will give you the foundation for data handling, charting, backtesting, and market analysis.

Step 5: Version Control with Git

Even if you're working solo, use Git. It lets you roll back bad changes, experiment safely, and keep your code history intact.

 # Initialize Git

git init

 # Commit your first version

git add .

git commit -m "Initial commit"

Link it to GitHub, GitLab, or Bitbucket so you have an off-site backup. Trust me, nothing stings like losing a month of work because your hard drive gave up.

Step 6: Set Up Your Broker API

Most algorithmic trading platforms require you to connect to your broker via API keys. For example:

- **Interactive Brokers** – IBKR API or IB Gateway
- **Alpaca** – Simple REST API for US stocks
- **Binance/CCXT** – For crypto

Store your API keys in environment variables or a .env file—never hard-code them in your scripts unless you enjoy the thrill of someone else trading with your money.

Step 7: Data Storage

You'll need a place to store historical and live market data:

- **Small scale** – CSV or SQLite
- **Larger scale** – PostgreSQL, MySQL, or MongoDB
- **Cloud-based** – AWS S3 for archival storage

Keep it organized. "final_final_updated_v3.csv" may sound fine now, but six months later, you won't remember what it was.

Step 8: Automation and Deployment

Eventually, you'll want your bot running 24/7 without your laptop staying on all night. Options:

- Local server or spare computer
- VPS (Virtual Private Server) – e.g., Linode, DigitalOcean, AWS EC2
- Docker – For a portable, replicable environment that runs anywhere

Step 9: Testing Before Going Live

Never trust your code without testing. Use paper trading or sandbox environments provided by brokers to ensure your bot behaves as expected.

And don't skip stress testing—simulate bad market conditions and see if your bot panics before you do.

Step 10: Document Everything

Write down how your environment is set up—versions, configurations, and dependencies. Future you will thank past you when you need to debug something at 2 a.m.

Final Thoughts

Setting up your development environment isn't glamorous, but it's the scaffolding that holds your trading system together. Get it right, and you can focus on building strategies instead of fixing technical headaches.

And remember—your bot is only as good as the environment it lives in. Build it a stable home, or it might start "acting out" like a teenager who just discovered energy drinks.

3.4 API Integration with Brokers and Data Feeds

When I first heard "API integration," I pictured something dramatic—like plugging my laptop into the stock exchange's mainframe while alarms went off in the background. In reality, it was me typing my API keys into a script at 2 a.m. and praying I didn't accidentally place a 10,000-share order for a penny stock.

What Is an API in Trading?

An API (Application Programming Interface) is basically the handshake between your trading bot and the outside world. It lets your code:

- Pull data from exchanges or data providers
- Send orders to your broker
- Check positions and account balances
- Subscribe to real-time market events

Without an API, you're stuck manually downloading CSVs or clicking "Buy" and "Sell" buttons like it's 1998.

Types of APIs You'll Encounter

Broker APIs – Provided by your broker for executing trades and managing accounts. Examples:

- Interactive Brokers API
- Alpaca API
- TD Ameritrade API
- Robinhood (Unofficial) APIs

Market Data APIs – Focused solely on delivering market prices and other stats. Examples:

- Polygon.io
- Alpha Vantage
- Yahoo Finance (via yfinance in Python)
- Quandl

Exchange APIs – For direct access to trading venues, especially in crypto. Examples:

- Binance API
- Coinbase Pro API
- Kraken API
- CCXT (library that unifies multiple exchange APIs)

Getting Started with API Integration

Step 1: Get Your API Keys

After signing up with your broker or data provider, you'll be given an API key and secret (sometimes also a passphrase). Treat these like the PIN to your bank account—if someone else has them, they can place trades in your name.

Step 2: Store Keys Securely

- Environment variables
- .env files (never upload to GitHub)
- Encrypted key storage

Bad idea: Hardcoding keys into your script.

Worse idea: Hardcoding keys into your script and emailing it to yourself.

Step 3: Install the API's SDK or Use REST Calls

Most brokers provide an SDK (software development kit) in Python, Java, or C++. If not, you can make direct REST API calls using Python's requests library or a wrapper like CCXT.

Pulling Data via API

Here's an example using Alpaca's Python SDK to get the latest Apple price:

```
from alpaca_trade_api import REST

api = REST('YOUR_API_KEY', 'YOUR_SECRET_KEY', base_url='https://paper-api.alpaca.markets')

quote = api.get_latest_quote('AAPL')

print(quote)
```

That's the API equivalent of walking into the market and asking, "So... what's Apple trading at?"

Sending Orders via API

For the same Alpaca API, a simple buy order might look like:

```
api.submit_order(

symbol='AAPL',

qty=10,

side='buy',

type='market',

time_in_force='gtc'

)
```

One line of code, and you're in the market. No mouse clicks required—just a mix of excitement and mild terror.

Streaming Data

Most APIs offer WebSocket connections for real-time updates. This is essential for low-latency strategies, as REST APIs can lag. For example, you can subscribe to live order book updates, price ticks, or trade executions.

Common Pitfalls

- **Rate Limits** – Most APIs limit how many requests you can send per minute. Exceed that, and you'll get blocked.
- **Paper vs. Live Trading** – Always start with the paper (simulated) environment to test your code safely.
- **Latency** – The speed of your API calls matters, especially in high-frequency strategies.
- **Error Handling** – If your bot crashes because the API didn't respond for 0.5 seconds, you've got bigger problems. Always code for timeouts and retries.

My Recommendations for Beginners

- Start with a broker that offers free paper trading and a simple API, like Alpaca or Interactive Brokers.
- Use a unified library like CCXT for crypto so you can switch exchanges without rewriting all your code.
- Build a "heartbeat" monitor—if your API connection drops, your bot should know and react.

The Bottom Line

API integration is your bot's lifeline to the market. Get it right, and you have a direct, flexible pipeline to execute trades and pull data exactly how you want it. Get it wrong, and your bot might sit idle... or worse, start trading like it's in a casino.

And trust me—watching your bot randomly buy $10,000 of Dogecoin because you mixed up "qty" and "price" in an API call is a special kind of pain you'll only make once.

3.5 Coding Your First Simple Strategy

I'll be honest—the first time I coded a trading strategy, I half-expected to wake up the next day and find I'd somehow become a billionaire in my sleep. Instead, I woke up to an error message that had been spamming my terminal for 7 hours straight. Lesson learned: simple does not mean sloppy.

Picking a Strategy to Start With

We're not going to reinvent the wheel here. For your first strategy, you want something:

- **Understandable** – You should be able to explain it in plain English.
- **Testable** – You can easily backtest it with historical data.
- **Rule-based** – No "gut feelings" allowed.

A moving average crossover is the classic beginner's choice. It's easy to code, easy to visualize, and a great way to learn the workflow.

The Moving Average Crossover Strategy

The idea:

- Calculate two moving averages—a short-term one and a long-term one.
- When the short-term MA crosses above the long-term MA → Buy signal.
- When it crosses below → Sell signal.

Example:

- **Short-term MA** = 50-day

- **Long-term MA** = 200-day

It's simple, but it will teach you the process from pulling data to executing trades.

Step 1: Getting Historical Data

Let's use yfinance to grab stock data for Apple:

```
import yfinance as yf

data = yf.download("AAPL", start="2020-01-01", end="2023-01-01")

print(data.head())
```

Step 2: Calculating Moving Averages

```
data['SMA50'] = data['Close'].rolling(window=50).mean()

data['SMA200'] = data['Close'].rolling(window=200).mean()
```

This creates two new columns in our dataset for the moving averages.

Step 3: Generating Buy/Sell Signals

```
data['Signal'] = 0

data['Signal'][50:] = \

(data['SMA50'][50:] > data['SMA200'][50:]).astype(int)

data['Position'] = data['Signal'].diff()
```

- **Signal = 1** → We're in a "buy" state.
- **Signal = 0** → We're in a "sell/neutral" state.
- **Position = 1** → Buy signal generated today.
- **Position = -1** → Sell signal generated today.

Step 4: Visualizing the Strategy

```
import matplotlib.pyplot as plt
plt.figure(figsize=(12,6))
plt.plot(data['Close'], label='Close Price', alpha=0.5)
plt.plot(data['SMA50'], label='50-Day SMA', alpha=0.9)
plt.plot(data['SMA200'], label='200-Day SMA', alpha=0.9)
plt.plot(data[data['Position'] == 1].index,
data['SMA50'][data['Position'] == 1],
'^', markersize=10, color='g', label='Buy Signal')
plt.plot(data[data['Position'] == -1].index,
data['SMA50'][data['Position'] == -1],
'v', markersize=10, color='r', label='Sell Signal')
plt.title('Moving Average Crossover Strategy')
plt.legend()
plt.show()
```

This chart will show you exactly where your buy and sell signals happened.

Step 5: Going Live (Carefully)

Once you're happy with backtesting results, you can connect this to your broker's API (from section 3.4) and replace your "signal" logic with actual trade execution calls. But—and I can't stress this enough—start with paper trading first.

Common Beginner Mistakes

- **Overfitting** – Don't tweak the MA periods just to make your backtest look perfect. That's curve fitting, and it will bite you in live trading.

- **Ignoring Costs** – Commissions and slippage can turn a "profitable" strategy into a losing one.

- **No Stop-Loss** – A simple crossover strategy can stay wrong for a very long time. Protect yourself.

The Big Picture

Coding your first strategy is less about finding the Holy Grail and more about learning the process:

1. Get data
2. Define clear rules
3. Backtest
4. Visualize results
5. Deploy cautiously

Once you've done it once, you can expand to more complex indicators, multiple assets, or risk management layers.

Closing Thought

Your first strategy is like your first car—it's probably not going to win races, but it will teach you how to drive without hitting a tree. And if it does hit a tree, better it's in the simulator than with your real trading account.

Chapter 4: Strategy Design Principles

Welcome to the strategy playground! Will your bot ride the trend like a surfer, scoop up mean reversions like a bargain shopper, or exploit price mismatches like a Wall Street ninja? Designing a strategy is like building a personality for your bot—quirks, boundaries, and all.

Here, we explore various categories of trading strategies, such as trend-following, mean-reversion, and arbitrage. The chapter guides readers through the process of identifying market inefficiencies, developing signal logic, and modeling risk versus reward. It also addresses the importance of setting constraints and clarifying assumptions to ensure realistic and functional strategy development.

4.1 Classifying Strategies: Trend, Mean Reversion, Arbitrage

When I first started out, I thought all trading strategies were basically the same: buy low, sell high. Turns out that's like saying all sports are the same because you "try to win." In reality, strategies fall into different families, each with its own philosophy, strengths, and quirks. And just like in sports, picking the wrong one for your personality can leave you frustrated—or worse, broke.

Trend-Following Strategies

Philosophy:

"The trend is your friend... until it bends." Trend-following assumes that prices tend to keep moving in the same direction for some period once a trend is established.

Examples:

- Moving average crossovers
- Breakouts above resistance levels
- Momentum-based strategies

How They Work:

You wait for evidence that a trend is forming (e.g., price moving above a moving average) and then jump on board, riding the wave until it shows signs of reversing.

Strengths:

- Can capture big moves

- Works well in markets with sustained trends (e.g., commodities, FX)

Weaknesses:

- Death by a thousand stop-outs in choppy, sideways markets
- Often late to enter and exit—never catching the exact top or bottom

Mean Reversion Strategies

Philosophy:

"What goes up must come down... and vice versa." Mean reversion assumes that prices oscillate around a fair value, and extreme deviations are temporary.

Examples:

- Bollinger Bands (buy when price hits the lower band, sell when it hits the upper)
- RSI oversold/overbought levels
- Pair trading between correlated assets

How They Work:

When a price moves too far from its "normal" range, you bet it will snap back. It's like betting your friend who stayed at the party too long will eventually come home

Strengths:

- Often yields frequent, small wins
- Can work well in range bound or stable markets

Weaknesses:

- Can get crushed if the "reversion" never happens (a.k.a. catching a falling knife)
- Requires solid risk management—those small wins can be wiped out by one big loss

Arbitrage Strategies

Philosophy:

"Why take risk when you can find free money?" Arbitrage seeks to exploit price differences between markets or instruments for a virtually risk-free profit—emphasis on "virtually," because in the real world, nothing is truly risk-free.

Examples:

- Spot-futures arbitrage (buying an asset and selling its futures contract)
- Cross-exchange crypto arbitrage
- Index arbitrage between ETF prices and underlying stocks

How They Work:

You identify situations where something is mispriced in one place relative to another, then buy low in one and sell high in the other—ideally at the same time.

Strengths:

- Can be very consistent in certain markets
- Minimal exposure to market direction

Weaknesses:

- Requires very low latency and high capital efficiency

- Opportunities are often tiny and vanish quickly
- High competition from institutions with deep pockets and faster tech

How to Choose

The strategy you gravitate toward depends on your:

- **Market Type:** Is it trending, range-bound, or highly fragmented?
- **Timeframe:** Are you trading intraday, swing, or long-term?
- **Resources:** Do you have low-latency access and advanced infrastructure?
- **Risk Appetite:** Can you stomach long losing streaks, or do you prefer small, steady gains?

Some traders mix these categories—e.g., a trend-following core with mean-reversion entries—to balance strengths and weaknesses.

The Big Picture

Classifying strategies is more than a naming exercise. It's about knowing what kind of game you're playing, the rules that govern it, and the traps that lie ahead. If you try to play chess using checkers rules, you're going to have a bad time.

Closing Thought

I once tried running a mean-reversion strategy in a strong trending market—it was like trying to surf by paddling in the opposite direction of the wave. Let's just say the market didn't "revert" so much as it steamrolled me for three straight weeks. Lesson learned: pick the right tool for the right job.

4.2 Identifying Market Inefficiencies

When I first heard the phrase "market inefficiency," I imagined it was like finding a $20 bill on the sidewalk—just sitting there, waiting for me to pick it up. Turns out, it's more like finding a $20 bill in a crowded stadium: by the time you see it, ten other people are already reaching for it, and one of them runs a 4.3-second forty-yard dash.

What Is a Market Inefficiency?

In theory, markets are "efficient"—meaning all available information is instantly reflected in prices. In practice, markets are run by humans (and their algorithms), which means they can be irrational, slow to react, or constrained by rules. These imperfections create small pockets of opportunity—what we call inefficiencies.

They can last milliseconds (in high-frequency environments) or months (in under-researched asset classes). Your job as an algo trader is to detect them before they vanish.

Common Types of Market Inefficiencies

Statistical Anomalies

- Patterns in price or volume that persist beyond randomness.
- Example: Certain assets performing better on Mondays, or momentum spillover from one day to the next.

Behavioral Biases

- Traders overreacting to news, panicking, or chasing trends.
- Example: Overbought sell-offs after mild bad news, followed by sharp reversals.

Information Delays

- Prices not adjusting instantly to new information because of slow dissemination or processing.
- **Example**: Small-cap earnings announcements taking hours to be fully reflected in price.

Market Structure Gaps

- Pricing mismatches due to how markets are set up.
- **Example:** Different exchanges quoting slightly different prices for the same asset.

Liquidity Imbalances

- Disproportionate buy/sell pressure causing short-term mispricings.
- **Example:** End-of-day rebalancing by large funds pushing prices temporarily away from fair value.

Tools for Detecting Inefficiencies

- **Statistical Analysis:** Run tests to see if observed patterns are significant or just noise.
- **Data Mining:** Scan large datasets for recurring setups, but beware of overfitting.
- **Event Studies:** Examine how prices react historically to specific events—earnings, economic releases, etc.
- **Order Flow Analysis:** Look at depth-of-market data to detect large, hidden orders influencing short-term movement.

- **Cross-Market Comparisons:** Spot pricing differences across related instruments or markets.

The Danger of "Finding" Inefficiencies That Aren't There

Just because something worked in your backtest doesn't mean it's a real inefficiency. Markets are noisy, and patterns often appear by chance. This is why you:

- Test on out-of-sample data.
- Validate with forward testing.
- Factor in costs—many "profitable" patterns vanish after accounting for commissions and slippage.

How Inefficiencies Evolve

Once an inefficiency becomes widely known, it usually shrinks or disappears. This is why algo traders constantly search for fresh edges. It's like fishing in a crowded pond—if everyone's using the same bait, the fish stop biting.

Some inefficiencies persist because they're tied to human behavior (fear and greed aren't going away anytime soon) or structural constraints (like certain market-making rules). But even those can mutate over time, so continuous monitoring is essential.

Practical Example

Let's say you notice that a certain tech stock tends to rally in the last 15 minutes of trading on Fridays.

- **Step 1:** Check if the effect holds across months and years.
- **Step 2:** Verify if it's specific to that stock or also appears in similar companies.

- **Step 3:** Factor in transaction costs—if the move is only 0.05% and your costs are 0.03%, your "edge" is basically a tip jar.

The Big Picture

Identifying inefficiencies is the bread and butter of algorithmic trading. But it's not about hunting unicorns—it's about finding small, repeatable edges and stacking them. One inefficiency won't make you rich, but ten well-managed ones might.

Closing Thought

If finding inefficiencies were easy, Wall Street interns would be retiring after their summer programs. In reality, the hunt is relentless, the competition fierce, and the window of opportunity often shorter than your morning coffee break. Which is why, when you do find one that works, you guard it like a secret family recipe.

4.3 Signal Generation Logic

When I was new to algo trading, I thought "signal generation" sounded glamorous—like Wall Street's version of NASA's mission control. In reality, it's less "launch the rocket" and more "check if the toaster is plugged in before pressing the button." But that toaster, if designed well, could print you money.

What Is Signal Generation?

At its core, signal generation is the decision-making engine of your trading system. It answers one simple but critical question: Do I buy, sell, or do nothing right now?

Everything else—data collection, analysis, execution—exists to support this moment. The signal is the bridge between your research idea and an actual trade in the market.

Inputs: What Feeds the Signal

Before a signal can be generated, your algorithm needs data to chew on. This can include:

- **Price Data:** Open, high, low, close (OHLC), tick data, volume.
- **Technical Indicators:** Moving averages, RSI, MACD, Bollinger Bands.
- **Fundamental Data:** Earnings reports, economic releases, analyst ratings.
- **Derived Metrics:** Volatility, momentum scores, sentiment indexes.
- **Market Microstructure:** Order book depth, bid-ask spread, trade flow.

Think of these as the "senses" of your algorithm—without them, it's trading blind.

Decision Rules

Once you have your inputs, you need logic to turn them into a decision. There are three main approaches:

Rule-Based Logic

- **Example:** "If 50-day moving average crosses above the 200-day moving average, generate a BUY signal."
- **Pros:** Transparent, easy to debug.
- **Cons:** Can be too rigid in changing market conditions.

Statistical Models

- **Example:** Linear regression predicting future returns based on past variables.
- **Pros:** Quantifiable, can measure confidence levels.
- **Cons:** Assumes past relationships hold in the future.

Machine Learning Models

- **Example:** Random forest classifier trained on historical data to predict up/down moves.
- **Pros:** Can capture complex, nonlinear relationships.
- **Cons:** Harder to interpret, risk of overfitting.

Types of Signals

- **Binary Signals:** Buy or sell, yes or no.

- **Probabilistic Signals:** Assign probabilities to outcomes (e.g., 70% chance of price increase).

- **Ranking Signals:** Rank multiple assets based on attractiveness, then choose top picks.

Filtering False Signals

Markets are noisy, and if you respond to every blip, you'll rack up transaction costs and headaches. Common filters include:

- **Minimum Thresholds:** Only trade if the predicted move exceeds a certain size.

- **Confirmation Indicators:** Require agreement from multiple indicators before acting.

- **Volatility Adjustments:** Avoid trading when volatility spikes unexpectedly.

Example: Simple Moving Average Crossover

Inputs: Closing prices over the last 200 days.

Logic:

- If short-term MA > long-term MA → BUY signal.

- If short-term MA < long-term MA → SELL signal.

Filter: Only act if the difference between MAs is greater than 0.5%.

This is the bread-and-butter type of signal logic for many beginner systems. It's simple, clear, and surprisingly effective in certain markets.

Implementation Tips

- **Keep It Modular:** Separate data handling, signal generation, and execution so you can tweak without breaking the whole system.

- **Test for Stability:** A signal that works only in specific historical periods is a red flag.

- **Don't Overcomplicate Early:** A simple, robust signal often beats an overly complex one that you can't explain.

The Big Picture

Signal generation is not about predicting the future with 100% accuracy. It's about identifying situations where the odds are tilted—even slightly—in your favor, then acting on them systematically.

Closing Thought

I once spent two months building a machine learning signal that I thought was genius—turned out, it was just very good at predicting yesterday's news. Sometimes, the best signal isn't the fanciest, it's the one that quietly makes money while you're not looking.

4.4 Risk and Reward Modeling

When I first started trading, I treated risk like the vegetables on my dinner plate—something I could just push to the side while I focused on the steak (profits). That worked for about a week, right up until the market served me a heaping plate of losses and no dessert. If you ignore risk, you're basically speed-running your way to blowing up your account.

Why Model Risk and Reward?

In trading, how much you make is only half the story. The other half—and arguably the more important one—is how much you can lose to make it. Risk and reward modeling is about quantifying both sides so you can decide whether a trade is worth taking before you even click "buy."

Think of it as a pre-nup with the market: you want to know what happens if things don't work out.

The Core Metrics

Risk per Trade

- **The dollar** (or percentage) amount you're willing to lose if you're wrong.
- **Common rule:** risk no more than 1–2% of your total capital on a single trade.

Reward-to-Risk Ratio (R:R)

- The potential profit divided by the potential loss.
- Example: Risking $100 for a chance to make $300 → R:R = 3:1.
- A higher R:R doesn't automatically mean better—it has to align with your win rate.

Win Rate

- The percentage of trades that are profitable.
- You can make money with a 30% win rate if your winners are big enough.

Expectancy

Formula:

Expectancy = (Win Rate × Average Win) – (Loss Rate × Average Loss)

This tells you the average amount you can expect to win (or lose) per trade over the long run.

Building a Risk/Reward Framework

Step 1: Define Risk Tolerances

Set a maximum portfolio drawdown you can stomach—both financially and emotionally. (If losing 15% of your account makes you lose sleep, don't set your risk to allow 15% drawdowns.)

Step 2: Determine Position Sizes

Use position-sizing formulas like the Kelly Criterion, fixed fractional method, or volatility-adjusted sizing to scale risk appropriately.

Step 3: Map Reward Scenarios

Estimate realistic profit targets based on historical data and volatility, not wishful thinking.

Step 4: Simulate Outcomes

Run Monte Carlo simulations or scenario analysis to see how your system behaves across thousands of hypothetical trade sequences.

Balancing the Equation

A system with a high win rate but terrible R:R can still be profitable, just as a low win rate with huge R:R can work too. The magic lies in pairing them correctly.

Example:

- **System A:** 80% win rate, R:R = 1:0.5 → Great until one bad loss wipes out ten wins.
- **System B:** 35% win rate, R:R = 3:1 → Uncomfortable losing streaks, but a few winners make up for it.

Hidden Pitfalls

- **Overestimating Reward:** Targets based on best-case scenarios rather than average outcomes will lead to disappointment.
- **Underestimating Risk:** Slippage, volatility spikes, and correlation between trades can magnify losses.
- **Ignoring Tail Risk:** Black swan events happen more often than we'd like to admit.

A Practical Example

Let's say:

- **Risk per trade** = 1% of $100,000 → $1,000.
- **Average win** = $2,500, average loss = $1,000.
- **Win rate = 40%.**

Expectancy = (0.40 × 2500) – (0.60 × 1000)

= 1000 – 600 = $400 per trade expected over time.

If you take 200 trades a year, that's about $80,000 expected—before transaction costs and taxes.

The Big Picture

Risk and reward modeling is not a "set it and forget it" exercise. Markets change, volatility shifts, and your strategy's performance can evolve. A good trader revisits their risk/reward assumptions regularly and adjusts before the market forces them to.

Closing Thought

I once met a trader who bragged about turning $10k into $100k in six months—impressive, until I learned he blew it all in a single week. Turns out, his "risk model" was just "hope for the best." Don't be that trader. In this game, managing the downside is the only way you get to stick around long enough to enjoy the upside.

4.5 Strategy Constraints and Assumptions

When I was younger in my trading career, I thought the market was a giant buffet—you just grab a plate (strategy) and load up on whatever looks good. Then reality hit: in trading, some of the "food" is missing, some spoils before you get there, and some is behind a "members only" sign. That's where constraints and assumptions come in—they define what's actually possible and what we believe to be true when designing a strategy.

Why Constraints and Assumptions Matter

A strategy without constraints is like a kid with unlimited candy money—it'll go wild until it crashes. Constraints keep your system grounded in reality, and assumptions define the environment your strategy is built to handle. Both are guardrails that prevent you from driving straight off a cliff.

Common Strategy Constraints

Capital Limitations

- How much money can you actually allocate to the strategy?
- A $5,000 account can't execute the same approach as a $50M fund—position sizing, diversification, and liquidity needs will be completely different.

Liquidity Requirements

- Can you enter and exit positions without moving the market too much?
- Small-cap stocks or exotic crypto pairs can look profitable on paper but be impossible to trade at scale.

Risk Parameters

- Maximum drawdown tolerance, per-trade risk limits, or volatility caps.
- Often expressed as "never lose more than X% in a single day/week/month."

Time Horizon

- Intraday? Swing trading? Long-term investing?
- Your execution style, data frequency, and holding costs will all be affected.

Market Access

- Not every trader can access every instrument or exchange—especially when regulations, broker limitations, or account type restrictions are involved.

Technology & Infrastructure

- Latency, computation speed, and API access may limit the complexity or frequency of trades.

Defining Assumptions

- Assumptions are the "rules of the world" your strategy lives in. Break them, and your model can collapse faster than a house of cards in a wind tunnel.

Common examples:

Market Regime Stability

- Assuming volatility levels, correlations, or liquidity conditions remain relatively stable.

Data Quality & Availability

- Assuming data is accurate, complete, and delivered on time.

Execution Certainty

- Assuming orders fill at expected prices (ignoring slippage can be dangerous).

Instrument Behavior

- Assuming that historical price patterns will repeat in the future.

Regulatory Consistency

- Assuming trading rules and tax treatment don't suddenly change.

Testing Constraints and Assumptions

- **Sensitivity Analysis:** Test how performance changes if assumptions shift (e.g., higher volatility, worse slippage).

- **Stress Testing:** Run the strategy through extreme but plausible scenarios—flash crashes, liquidity droughts, sudden correlation breakdowns.

- **Scaling Simulations:** See if the strategy still works with larger position sizes or portfolio capital.

The Danger of Hidden Assumptions

Many strategies fail because they're built on unspoken assumptions. For example, a mean reversion strategy might quietly assume that central banks will always step in during a crisis—then 2020 comes along and smashes that theory in the face.

A Practical Example

Let's say you design an intraday equity strategy with:

- **Constraint:** Maximum $2M position size per stock.

- **Assumption:** Bid-ask spread stays under 2 cents during normal market hours.

You backtest it and it looks amazing. Then, earnings season hits, spreads widen to 10 cents, and your PnL gets shredded. The problem wasn't the code—it was the assumption that spreads would always stay tight.

The Big Picture

Constraints aren't there to limit your creativity—they keep you from wasting time on impossible ideas. Assumptions aren't bad, but they need to be explicit, tested, and updated as markets change. The best traders I know constantly challenge their own assumptions and adapt constraints to reality, not wishful thinking.

Closing Thought

Think of constraints and assumptions like the frame and foundation of a house. If they're solid, you can paint the walls any color you like. But if you assume the ground will never move and it turns out you're building on quicksand, well... let's just say the market will be happy to hand you the demolition bill.

Chapter 5: Backtesting and Validation

Ah, backtesting—the time machine for your trading ideas. It's all fun and games until you realize your "genius" strategy only worked in 2012 on Tuesdays when it rained. Before you unleash your bot on live markets, let's make sure it doesn't suffer from selective memory or fortune-teller syndrome.

This chapter emphasizes the critical role of historical testing in strategy validation. It walks through building a robust backtesting framework, avoiding common pitfalls like lookahead bias and survivorship bias, and selecting appropriate performance metrics. Readers will also learn about advanced validation techniques such as walk-forward analysis and cross-validation.

5.1 Importance of Historical Testing

When I wrote my very first trading strategy, I was convinced I'd cracked the code. It was simple, elegant, and—most importantly—completely untested. So naturally, I went live with real money. The market immediately taught me that my "brilliant" system was about as effective as using a chocolate teapot. That's when I learned the value of historical testing.

What Is Historical Testing?

Historical testing—often called backtesting—is the process of applying your strategy to past market data to see how it would have performed. It's not about predicting the future with certainty, but about stress-testing your logic against what's already happened.

Think of it as a flight simulator for your trading system. You can crash and burn without actually losing your shirt.

Why It Matters

Proof of Concept

Backtesting lets you validate that your idea works outside your imagination.

Performance Metrics

You'll learn key stats like win rate, average return, drawdown, and Sharpe ratio before risking capital.

Identifying Weak Spots

Testing over years of data can reveal where your system struggles—low volatility, high volatility, trending markets, choppy markets, and so on.

Confidence Building

Knowing your system has survived multiple market cycles helps you stick to it during rough patches.

The Right Way to Backtest

Use High-Quality Data

Garbage in, garbage out. Inaccurate or incomplete data leads to misleading results.

Include Transaction Costs

Commissions, slippage, and fees can turn a "profitable" backtest into a losing reality.

Avoid Overfitting

Don't tweak your parameters to perfectly match past data—that just makes your strategy a history expert, not a future performer.

Test Across Market Conditions

Make sure your strategy can handle both sunny days and hurricanes.

Account for Survivorship Bias

Use data that includes delisted stocks, not just the winners that are still trading.

Common Pitfalls

- **Cherry-Picking Time Frames:** Choosing periods that make your system look good is just lying to yourself.

- **Ignoring Out-of-Sample Testing:** If you don't test on data your system hasn't seen, you risk building something that only works on the dataset you trained it on.

- **Neglecting Practical Constraints:** Your backtest might assume instant execution with no liquidity issues—reality will disagree.

An Example Scenario

Let's say your backtest shows:

- **Win rate:** 55%
- **Reward-to-risk:** 2:1
- **Max drawdown:** 12%
- **Annualized return:** 18%

That's not just numbers—it's a map of what to expect. And when the strategy hits a losing streak, you can compare your current performance to historical behavior to see if it's within normal limits or if something's broken.

The Reality Check

Historical testing isn't about proving your strategy will make money—it's about increasing the probability that it can. Markets evolve, so your testing should be ongoing. Treat it as a tool for learning and refining, not a one-time stamp of approval.

Closing Thought

Skipping historical testing is like buying a parachute without checking if it's been folded correctly. Sure, maybe it'll work when you jump, but if it doesn't... well, gravity is going to settle the debate real quick.

5.2 Creating Robust Backtesting Frameworks

When I first started building backtests, my "framework" was basically a spreadsheet, a prayer, and a lot of wishful thinking. It worked fine for testing one or two trades—until I realized I'd "accidentally" forgotten to include transaction costs, realistic execution, and a little thing called market reality. The results looked amazing, but they were about as real as a Hollywood hacker scene. That's when I learned the importance of a proper backtesting framework.

What Makes a Backtesting Framework "Robust"?

A robust backtesting framework doesn't just tell you how much money you would have made—it gives you a realistic, unbiased, and repeatable way to evaluate a strategy under conditions that resemble actual trading.

It should:

1. Handle large datasets efficiently.
2. Model trades with realistic constraints.
3. Capture all relevant metrics for decision-making.
4. Be flexible enough to test multiple strategies and parameters.

Key Components of a Solid Backtesting Setup

Clean, High-Quality Data

- Your framework should be able to detect and handle missing data, outliers, and bad ticks.

- Support multiple data types (minute, tick, daily) depending on your strategy's time frame.

Accurate Trade Simulation

- Include bid-ask spreads, slippage, and realistic order types.
- Simulate partial fills if liquidity is an issue.

Parameter Management

- Allow easy testing of different parameters without rewriting code.
- Support walk-forward testing to avoid overfitting.

Risk & Performance Metrics

- Calculate key stats: win rate, Sharpe ratio, max drawdown, profit factor, exposure time.
- Make them easy to compare across strategies.

Modularity

- Keep strategy logic separate from data handling and execution simulation.
- This makes it easier to upgrade or swap components without breaking the whole thing.

Out-of-Sample Testing

- Build the ability to split data into in-sample (for strategy development) and out-of-sample (for validation).

The Process of Building One

Define the Scope

- Decide what markets, instruments, and timeframes you'll support.

Set the Data Pipeline

- Create a reliable method for loading, cleaning, and storing historical data.

Develop the Execution Engine

- This is where you simulate entering and exiting trades based on signals.

Add Risk & Portfolio Management

- Position sizing, leverage limits, diversification rules—all built into the framework.

Integrate Performance Reporting

- Include visualizations: equity curves, drawdown charts, trade distribution histograms.

Testing Your Backtesting

Yes, you actually have to backtest your backtester. I know it sounds ridiculous, but I've seen frameworks spit out perfect equity curves simply because of a small coding error. Run controlled tests with known outcomes to make sure your system isn't cheating (e.g., future-looking bias).

Practical Example

Let's say we're building in Python. A modular framework might have:

- data.py for importing and cleaning historical data.
- strategy.py for your trading logic.
- execution.py for simulating trades with realistic fills.
- metrics.py for calculating and reporting stats.
- runner.py to tie it all together.

This structure lets you swap strategies without touching the rest of the system, making experimentation much faster.

Common Mistakes to Avoid

- **Mixing strategy code with data cleaning:** Makes debugging a nightmare.

- **Ignoring computational efficiency:** Tick data on a 10-year range will crush a slow framework.

- **Not validating results independently:** Always double-check numbers with another tool.

The Big Picture

A good backtesting framework is like a good kitchen—you can have the best recipe in the world, but if the kitchen is dirty, disorganized, and missing tools, your meal will be a disaster. Building something clean, reliable, and flexible upfront saves a ton of headaches later.

Closing Thought

If you're serious about algorithmic trading, your backtesting framework isn't just a tool—it's your truth machine. And trust me, the market will punish you if you feed yourself comfortable lies. Better to have your framework slap you in the face now than have the market do it later—it's cheaper, and you don't have to explain it to your broker.

5.3 Avoiding Lookahead and Survivorship Bias

When I first heard the term "lookahead bias," I pictured a trader with psychic powers, calmly buying stocks before news hits. Unfortunately, that's not a skill—it's a mistake. **Same with survivorship bias:** if you only look at companies that are still alive, you're ignoring the graveyard full of bankrupt tickers. Both will make your backtests look amazing right up until the moment you trade them live... and the market takes all your lunch money.

What Is Lookahead Bias?

Lookahead bias happens when your strategy uses information in a backtest that would not have been available at the time of the trade.

Example:

If your algorithm buys a stock at 10:00 AM because of a price reported at 10:05 AM, congratulations—you've just built a time machine in your code. Unfortunately, it only works in backtests.

How It Sneaks In:

- Using daily closing prices to trigger trades "on the same day"
- Using future earnings reports, analyst upgrades, or economic data without accounting for release time
- Misaligned data timestamps between indicators and price data

What Is Survivorship Bias?

Survivorship bias occurs when you only test your strategy on assets that still exist, ignoring those that were delisted, went bankrupt, or merged out of existence.

Example:

Testing a stock-picking strategy on today's S&P 500 constituents without including companies that were in the index in the past but failed. You'll get artificially high returns because you've removed the losers from history.

How It Sneaks In:

- Using a dataset from your broker that excludes dead tickers
- Backtesting ETFs without accounting for changing holdings over time
- Using "current" index membership lists for historical periods

Why These Biases Are Dangerous

Overstated Performance

Both biases make your strategy appear much more profitable than it actually is.

False Confidence

You'll think your system is bulletproof... right before reality smashes it.

Poor Risk Estimation

Without the losers in your dataset or the delays in real data, you'll underestimate drawdowns and volatility.

How to Avoid Lookahead Bias

Align Data Properly

- Make sure your indicators and signals are calculated using only information available at that exact time.

Simulate Delays

- If an economic report is released at 8:30 AM, your strategy shouldn't act on it at 8:29.

Test With Intraday Data

- This helps avoid using end-of-day info for intraday decisions.

How to Avoid Survivorship Bias

Use Survivorship-Bias-Free Data

- Buy datasets that include delisted securities. Many professional data vendors offer this.

Replicate Historical Indexes

- Make sure your backtest uses the actual historical constituents for each date, not the current list.

Track Corporate Actions

- Adjust prices for splits, mergers, and dividends to reflect actual trading conditions.

A Practical Illustration

Imagine you backtest a strategy on the S&P 500 from 2000–2020 using only today's constituents. You might find a 12% annual return with moderate drawdowns. But if you include all the companies that were in the index during that time but failed, that return might drop to 6%—and drawdowns double. That's the difference between a system you can trade and a system that just looked good in fantasy land.

Testing Your Backtest

One trick I use: run your strategy on a dataset you know has survivorship bias, then run it again on a bias-free dataset. The difference will give you a sense of how much "cheating" was happening. Same for lookahead bias—insert artificial delays and see how much performance changes.

The Big Picture

Bias-free backtesting is less glamorous because it usually makes your strategy's performance look worse. But that's a good thing. Better to know the ugly truth now than learn it while watching your account balance vanish in real time.

Closing Thought

Lookahead and survivorship bias are like Photoshop for backtests—they make everything look flawless. The only problem? When you see the unedited version (your real trading results), it's a shock. And trust me, the market doesn't hand out airbrush tools.

5.4 Performance Metrics: Sharpe, Sortino, and More

When I first started trading, I judged strategies the same way I judged pizza—by the size of the slice. If it made a lot of money, it was "good." Turns out, just looking at returns is like rating a roller coaster only by how tall it is without asking how many people threw up along the way. That's where performance metrics come in.

Why Metrics Matter

A strategy can have great returns but be completely untradeable because of massive drawdowns, volatility, or risk exposure. Performance metrics give you a fuller picture, showing not just how much a strategy made, but how it made it.

Sharpe Ratio

The Sharpe ratio measures risk-adjusted returns—basically, how much excess return you're getting for each unit of risk.

Formula:

$$Sharpe - \frac{R_p - R_f}{\sigma_p}$$

Where:

- R_p = Portfolio return
- R_f = Risk-free rate
- σ_p = Standard deviation of portfolio returns

Why It Matters:

A Sharpe of 1.0 is decent, 2.0 is very good, and 3.0+ means you're either a genius or your data is lying to you.

Sortino Ratio

The Sortino ratio is like the Sharpe's less judgmental cousin—it only penalizes you for downside volatility.

Formula:

$$Sortino = \frac{R_p - R_f}{\sigma_{downside}}$$

Why It Matters:

If your strategy has high upside swings but low downside swings, the Sortino will look better than the Sharpe. Traders love it because it focuses on "bad" volatility instead of all volatility.

Max Drawdown

Max drawdown (MDD) is the largest peak-to-trough drop in your portfolio value during the backtest.

Why It Matters:

A strategy with a 50% max drawdown needs a 100% gain just to break even. MDD tells you how much pain you'll need to tolerate before the gains arrive—if they arrive at all.

Calmar Ratio

The Calmar ratio compares annual returns to max drawdown:

$$Calmar = \frac{\text{Annual Return}}{\text{Max Drawdown}}$$

Why It Matters:

It rewards strategies that deliver high returns without gut-wrenching drawdowns.

Win Rate & Profit Factor

- **Win Rate:** Percentage of trades that end up profitable. High win rates aren't always good if losses are huge when they occur.

- **Profit Factor:** Total profit divided by total loss. Anything above 1.5 is generally considered solid.

Expectancy

Expectancy tells you the average amount you can expect to win (or lose) per trade.

Formula:

$$Expectancy = (P_{win} \times AvgWin) - (P_{loss} \times AvgLoss)$$

Equity Curve & Volatility

Sometimes numbers don't tell the whole story. Looking at the shape of your equity curve helps you see periods of stagnation, sudden spikes, or slow bleeding drawdowns.

Putting It All Together

I like to keep a performance "dashboard" that shows:

- Sharpe ratio
- Sortino ratio
- Max drawdown
- Calmar ratio
- Win rate

- Profit factor
- Equity curve chart

If a strategy only looks good by one metric and terrible by the rest, that's a red flag.

Practical Example

Let's compare two strategies:

Metric	Strategy A	Strategy B
Annual Return	20%	18%
Sharpe Ratio	1.1	2.0
Sortino Ratio	1.6	3.0
Max Drawdown	30%	10%
Calmar Ratio	0.66	1.8

Even though Strategy A has slightly higher returns, Strategy B is the clear winner when you factor in risk and consistency.

The Big Picture

The point of these metrics isn't to make your backtest look pretty—it's to tell you the truth. High returns without proper risk measurement are like driving 200 mph without a seatbelt: sure, it's fun until you hit a wall.

Closing Thought

Performance metrics are your trading lie detectors. Ignore them, and you'll end up trusting strategies that will betray you faster than a free trial that demands your credit card.

5.5 Walk-Forward Analysis and Cross-Validation

When I was a rookie trader, I thought one great backtest meant my strategy was ready for the big leagues. That's like assuming you're ready for the Olympics after winning a friendly race against your grandma. Sure, it feels good, but the competition out there is... let's just say less forgiving. Walk-forward analysis and cross-validation are how we make sure our strategies can actually survive in the wild.

Why We Need More Than a Single Backtest

A single backtest, even if bias-free, is still just one test on one slice of history. It's easy to unknowingly overfit your parameters to that specific dataset. Walk-forward analysis and cross-validation give you multiple rounds of "auditions" to see if your strategy can handle different market conditions without falling apart.

Walk-Forward Analysis (WFA)

Walk-forward analysis is essentially training and testing your strategy in rolling time windows.

How It Works:

- **Pick a period of historical data** (say, 2000–2020).
- **Split it into an in-sample period** (used for optimization) and an out-of-sample period (used for testing).
- Optimize your strategy on the in-sample data.
- **Run it** (without changes) on the out-of-sample data.
- **Roll the window forward** (e.g., shift one year ahead) and repeat.

Why It's Good:

- Mimics how strategies are developed and then traded in real time.
- Tests your system across changing conditions.
- Reduces overfitting risk.

Example:

- **Train:** 2000–2005 → Test: 2006
- **Train:** 2001–2006 → Test: 2007
- **Train:** 2002–2007 → Test: 2008

...and so on until you cover the full dataset.

Cross-Validation

Cross-validation, more common in machine learning, can also be applied to trading. Instead of splitting your dataset chronologically (like in WFA), you split it into k-folds—chunks of data that you rotate between training and testing.

Why It's Good:

- Gives you a better average estimate of performance.
- Ensures your strategy is robust across multiple subsets of your data.

The Catch:

In trading, you need to preserve the time order of events. So, we can't randomly shuffle data like we do in normal machine learning—otherwise, you get lookahead bias. Instead, we use time-series cross-validation that respects chronological order.

Comparing the Two

- **Walk-Forward Analysis:** Best for mimicking "develop, deploy, and monitor" cycles in real life.
- **Cross-Validation:** Best for evaluating stability of parameters and reducing the risk of overfitting when you have less data.

Many pros use both—WFA for realism and time-series cross-validation for parameter robustness.

Practical Tips

Keep In-Sample Periods Realistic

If your in-sample period is too short, you risk overfitting. Too long, and you may miss recent market changes.

Track Performance Across All Runs

Don't cherry-pick your best walk-forward run. Look at average returns, drawdowns, and consistency.

Monitor Parameter Stability

If your "optimal" parameters change wildly between runs, your system may not be robust.

Simulate Realistic Constraints

Include slippage, commissions, and execution delays in every test.

A Quick Illustration

Let's say you have a moving average crossover strategy. You run a walk-forward test over 20 years, optimizing the fast/slow periods each time. If your average out-of-sample Sharpe ratio is consistently above 1.5 and max drawdowns stay reasonable, that's a good sign. If it's profitable in only a couple of years and crashes in the rest, it's not the market's fault—it's your system's.

The Big Picture

WFA and cross-validation aren't about squeezing more returns out of your strategy—they're about making sure it's actually tradeable long-term. Without them, you risk falling in love with a curve-fit masterpiece that collapses the moment market conditions shift.

Closing Thought

Skipping walk-forward analysis is like marrying someone after just one good date—you might think you've found "the one," but reality can hit hard when the honeymoon period ends. And unlike relationships, there's no alimony in trading—just your account balance waving goodbye.

Chapter 6: Risk Management and Position Sizing

Imagine letting your bot bet the entire account on a hunch—it's like giving your dog your credit card and hoping it doesn't buy 50 tennis balls. Risk management isn't optional; it's survival. Trust us, nothing humbles like a rogue trade.

In this chapter, we examine the different dimensions of trading risk, from individual trade exposure to overall portfolio risk. Concepts such as the Kelly Criterion, fixed fractional sizing, and drawdown control are introduced. The chapter also covers stop-loss mechanisms, take-profit tactics, and capital preservation techniques vital for long-term success.

6.1 Types of Trading Risks

When I first got into trading, I thought the only risk was "losing money." Simple, right? But that's like saying the only danger in hiking is "falling off a cliff." Sure, it's a big one, but you can also twist an ankle, get eaten by mosquitoes, or wander into a bear's lunch zone. In trading, risks come in many flavors—and some are sneakier than others.

1. Market Risk

The big one. This is the risk that the market simply moves against your position. If you're long and prices drop, you lose. If you're short and prices rise, you lose.

Why It's Unavoidable:

Market risk is the ocean—you can't avoid waves, but you can learn to surf without drowning.

How to Manage It:

- Position sizing
- Stop losses
- Hedging (if appropriate)

2. Liquidity Risk

Ever try to sell something on an online marketplace and realize no one wants it? That's liquidity risk—except in trading, "no buyers" or "no sellers" means you might not get out of your trade at a fair price, or at all.

When It Hurts Most:

- In small-cap stocks
- During low-volume trading hours

- In sudden market panics

Mitigation:

- Trade in liquid instruments
- Watch the bid-ask spread
- Avoid over-sized positions in thin markets

3. Execution Risk

Your strategy says "buy now," but by the time your order hits the market, the price has moved. Or worse, your broker's system glitches.

Causes:

- Latency (delays in order transmission)
- Slippage
- Technical outages

Mitigation:

- Use reliable infrastructure
- Test broker APIs under load
- Keep backup execution methods

4. Credit Risk

This is the risk that the counterparty in your trade—like a broker or clearinghouse—fails to deliver on their obligations.

Example:

If your broker goes bankrupt mid-trade, you might not get your money back (looking at you, Lehman Brothers 2008).

Mitigation:

- Use well-capitalized brokers
- Check regulatory protections (e.g., SIPC in the US)

5. Operational Risk

This isn't about markets—it's about you and your systems. Fat-finger errors, wrong code deployment, or even forgetting a "minus" sign in your algorithm.

Real-Life Horror:

I once ran a strategy where I mixed up position size variables—accidentally placing trades 10x larger than intended. My heart rate could've powered a small city.

Mitigation:

- Double-check code before deployment
- Implement fail-safes and sanity checks
- Use simulation environments

6. Model Risk

Your beautifully backtested strategy is wrong—either because of flawed assumptions, outdated data, or simply because the market changed.

The Trap:

Mistaking "historical patterns" for "future guarantees."

Mitigation:

- Continually revalidate your models
- Avoid overfitting
- Use multiple strategies for diversification

7. Regulatory and Compliance Risk

Markets don't just have rules—they have rulebooks thicker than a Thanksgiving turkey. Break one (intentionally or not), and you can face fines or account freezes.

Examples:

- Trading halts
- Pattern day trader rules
- Short-selling bans during crises

Mitigation:

- Stay updated on regulations for your markets
- Work with brokers who provide compliance guidance

8. Psychological Risk

Yes, your own brain can be a risk factor. Overconfidence, revenge trading, fear of missing out (FOMO)—all these mental traps can lead to bad decisions.

Mitigation:

- Follow a written trading plan
- Automate execution when possible
- Review trades objectively

Why Knowing the Risks Matters

It's tempting to focus only on potential profits, but understanding risks lets you design systems that survive. You can't control the market, but you can control how exposed you are to its dangers.

Closing Thought

Ignoring trading risks is like going to a buffet and ignoring the "spicy" labels—sure, you might get lucky, but more often than not, you'll end up sweating, panicking, and wondering why you ever thought it was a good idea.

6.2 Portfolio Risk vs. Trade Risk

Early in my career, I thought risk management was just about "not losing too much on one trade." Then I learned the hard way that you can have a bunch of "safe" trades and still end up with a portfolio that blows up faster than microwave popcorn left unattended. That's when I realized—trade risk and portfolio risk are related, but not the same animal.

Trade Risk – The Microscope View

Definition:

Trade risk is the potential loss you face on a single position if the market moves against you.

Example:

You buy 100 shares of a $50 stock with a stop loss at $48. That's $2 per share risk, or $200 total.

Why It Matters:

- Sets boundaries for individual trades
- Helps size positions correctly
- Keeps single mistakes from sinking your account

How to Manage It:

- Use stop losses (hard or mental)
- Limit risk per trade to a small percentage of total capital (e.g., 1–2%)
- Adjust position sizes based on volatility

Portfolio Risk – The Big Picture

Definition:

Portfolio risk is the total potential loss your entire set of positions could face due to market moves, correlations, or systemic events.

Example:

You've got five different tech stocks that each have "only" $200 trade risk. But if the tech sector crashes, they might all tank together—and suddenly you're down $1,000 in a blink.

Why It Matters:

- Multiple trades can be correlated without you realizing
- Market shocks can hit every position at once
- Diversification isn't just about holding more names—it's about holding different kinds of risk

How to Manage It:

- Diversify across sectors, asset classes, and strategies
- Monitor correlation between positions
- Limit total exposure to highly correlated trades

How They Work Together

Think of trade risk as making sure each wave doesn't knock you down, and portfolio risk as making sure a tsunami doesn't wipe out your entire beach house.

Even if you control trade risk perfectly, ignoring portfolio risk can lead to catastrophic losses. Conversely, if you're diversified at the portfolio level but take reckless individual trades, you can bleed out one bad position at a time.

Practical Steps to Balance Both

Set Trade-Level Limits

Decide the max % of account equity you're willing to risk on a single trade.

Set Portfolio-Level Limits

Cap your total sector or strategy exposure so one theme can't sink you.

Stress-Test Your Portfolio

Simulate scenarios like 5% drop in a sector, interest rate hikes, or sudden volatility spikes.

Monitor Correlation

Tools like correlation matrices help you see hidden clustering of risk.

A Quick Story

I once ran a "diversified" portfolio of 12 positions... except 9 of them were just different flavors of the same tech momentum trade. When the sector tanked, it was like watching 9 dominos fall in slow motion—except they were all holding my money.

Closing Thought

Managing trade risk without portfolio risk is like wearing a life jacket in a swimming pool but refusing to check the weather before going deep-sea sailing. Sure, you might float for a while—but the storm's still coming.

6.3 Kelly Criterion and Fixed Fractional Positioning

When I first heard about the Kelly Criterion, someone told me it was the "mathematically perfect way to bet." I was intrigued—until I ran it on one of my early trading systems and the formula basically told me, "Go all in, cowboy." Turns out, math can be right and terrifying at the same time. That's why, in real trading, we usually tone Kelly down a notch and pair it with saner methods like fixed fractional positioning.

The Kelly Criterion – Gambling Math for Grown-Ups

What It Is:

The Kelly Criterion comes from information theory and gambling mathematics. It tells you exactly what fraction of your capital to risk per trade to maximize long-term growth.

The Formula:

$$f^* = \frac{bp - q}{b}$$

Where:

- f^* = optimal fraction of capital to risk
- b = net odds received (profit per unit risk)
- p = probability of winning
- q = probability of losing (1 – p)

Example:

If you win 55% of the time and your wins are equal to your losses (1:1 reward/risk), then:

$$f^* = \frac{1 \times 0.55 - 0.45}{1} = 0.10$$

So you'd risk 10% of your capital per trade. Sounds nice until you realize that's huge risk for real money.

Why Kelly Can Be Dangerous in Trading

- **Requires Accurate Win Probability** – If your estimate is wrong, you can massively over-risk.
- **Volatility** – Full Kelly sizing can create huge equity swings.
- **Changing Market Conditions** – Your "perfect" inputs today may be garbage tomorrow.

Pro Tip:

Many traders use half-Kelly or quarter-Kelly to reduce volatility and account for uncertainty.

Fixed Fractional Positioning – The Simpler Cousin

What It Is:

You risk a fixed percentage of your capital on each trade—regardless of your win rate or odds.

Example:

You decide to risk 2% of your account per trade. With a $50,000 account, your max risk per trade is $1,000.

If your stop loss is $5 away from your entry, you can buy:

$$\frac{1000}{5} = 200 \text{ shares}$$

Benefits:

- Simple to calculate

- Keeps risk consistent
- Adapts automatically as account size changes

Downside:

- Doesn't account for edge strength—your best strategies get the same allocation as weaker ones

Combining the Two

Some traders blend them—using the Kelly formula to estimate "edge-adjusted" risk and then capping it at a safer fixed fractional limit. For example:

- Kelly says risk 8%
- You cap at 2% per trade for sanity

When to Use Which

- **Kelly Criterion:** When you have a proven, stable edge with accurate stats (common in market making or HFT).
- **Fixed Fractional:** When you want a robust, easy-to-implement risk sizing rule that works in most conditions.

My Personal Take

I like Kelly as a theoretical compass—it shows you where the mathematically optimal point might be. But in the real, messy world of trading, I size more conservatively using fixed fractional rules. If Kelly says "risk big," I smile, nod, and still play it safe.

Closing Thought

Kelly is like that friend who tells you to bet your whole paycheck on the "sure thing" at the horse track—he might be right, but you'll sleep a lot better using fixed fractional and buying dinner after you win, not before.

6.4 Stop-Loss and Take-Profit Mechanisms

When I was a rookie, I treated stop losses like the vegetables on my dinner plate—technically there for my health, but easy to ignore if the steak looked good. And take profits? I figured, "Why limit myself when the market could keep going my way?" Fast forward a few painful lessons later, and now I treat stop-loss and take-profit orders like oxygen masks on a plane—you hope you never need them, but you'd better know where they are.

The Purpose of a Stop-Loss

Definition:

A stop-loss order automatically exits a trade if the price moves against you by a set amount. It's your emergency brake.

Why It Matters:

- Prevents catastrophic losses
- Enforces discipline
- Protects you from emotional decision-making in the heat of the moment

Types of Stop-Loss Orders:

1. **Fixed Price Stop** – You pick a specific price to exit.
2. **Percentage Stop** – Exits when price moves a set percentage against you.
3. **Volatility-Based Stop** – Adjusted based on market volatility (e.g., ATR stops).
4. **Trailing Stop** – Moves up (or down, for shorts) as price moves in your favor, locking in profits.

The Purpose of a Take-Profit

Definition:

A take-profit order automatically closes your position when a set profit target is reached. It's your cash register.

Why It Matters:

- Locks in gains before the market turns
- Prevents greed from keeping you in too long
- Helps maintain consistent results

Types of Take-Profit Orders:

1. **Fixed Target** – A set price where you exit.
2. **Percentage Target** – Exit after a set % gain.
3. **Multiple Targets** – Take partial profits at multiple levels.
4. **Trailing Profit Target** – Similar to trailing stops, but aimed at capturing more upside while protecting gains.

Common Mistakes with Stops and Targets

- **Too Tight Stops:** Get triggered by normal market noise.
- **Too Wide Stops:** Risk more than your plan allows.
- **No Stops at All:** Basically asking the market to test your pain threshold.
- **Arbitrary Targets:** Choosing profit levels without reference to volatility, support/resistance, or risk/reward ratio.

Best Practices

Base Them on Data, Not Guesswork

Use historical volatility or backtesting to determine optimal distances.

Align with Risk/Reward Ratios

Aim for at least 1:2 (risk $1 to make $2).

Don't Move Your Stops Without a Good Reason

"Good reason" doesn't mean "I hope it turns around."

Review and Adjust Over Time

Markets change—your stops and targets should too.

How They Work Together

Think of stops and profits like guardrails on a mountain road. The stop-loss keeps you from tumbling off a cliff, while the take-profit keeps you from endlessly circling the mountain hoping the view gets better.

Many traders use both:

- Enter trade
- Place stop-loss to limit downside
- Place take-profit to secure upside
- Let the orders do the work

My Approach

I usually combine a volatility-based stop with either a fixed or trailing take-profit. This way, I protect against sudden drops but also let winners run when the market has momentum. If my system says there's potential for more upside, the trailing mechanism keeps me in just long enough without giving too much back.

Closing Thought

Trading without stop-losses or take-profits is like driving without brakes or a destination—you might feel free for a while, but sooner or later, physics (or the market) will remind you who's in charge.

6.5 Drawdown Management and Capital Preservation

When I first started trading, I thought "drawdown" was just a temporary dip that you could "wait out" if you believed in your trades. Spoiler: the market does not care about your beliefs. I once "waited out" a position so long it became a long-term investment purely by accident. That was my crash course in why managing drawdowns is not optional—it's survival.

What Is a Drawdown?

Definition:

A drawdown is the percentage decline from your account's peak equity to its lowest point before a new high is reached.

Example:

If your account peaks at $100,000 and later drops to $80,000, you've experienced a 20% drawdown.

Why It Matters:

- Large drawdowns require disproportionately higher returns to recover. (A 50% drawdown needs a 100% gain to break even.)
- They mess with your head, tempting you into bad decisions.
- Excessive drawdowns often precede traders quitting entirely.

Capital Preservation – The Golden Rule

If there's one rule in trading that beats all others, it's this: Don't lose big. Making money is exciting, but keeping it is the real game.

Strategies for Managing Drawdowns

1. Position Sizing Discipline

- Keep risk per trade small enough to prevent a string of losses from wrecking your account.
- The smaller the per-trade risk, the shallower the drawdowns.

2. Daily/Weekly Loss Limits

- If you hit a set loss limit in a day or week, stop trading.
- This prevents overtrading while emotional.

3. Diversification

- Spread capital across uncorrelated markets and strategies.
- This cushions your portfolio when one area gets hit.

4. Dynamic Exposure Reduction

- Reduce position size or halt new trades during a drawdown period until equity stabilizes.

5. Regular Performance Reviews

- Identify whether a drawdown is just bad luck or a sign your strategy stopped working.

Avoiding the Death Spiral

The "death spiral" is when losses trigger emotional decisions, which cause more losses, which trigger worse decisions. Signs you might be entering it:

- Increasing position sizes to "make it back" faster.
- Abandoning your trading rules out of frustration.
- Jumping into random trades to chase recent winners.

Capital preservation is as much about protecting your mental capital as your financial one.

The Recovery Math Problem

Here's the part most traders underestimate:

- 10% loss → need 11.1% gain to recover
- 20% loss → need 25% gain to recover
- 50% loss → need 100% gain to recover

The deeper you go, the harder the climb. That's why the best traders avoid falling too far in the first place.

My Approach

I set a maximum acceptable drawdown at both the strategy level and portfolio level—usually in the 15–20% range. If I hit that, I stop, reassess, and scale down. I also build "circuit breakers" into my systems that cut exposure if losses breach a daily or weekly threshold.

Final Word

Think of capital preservation like keeping oxygen tanks for deep diving—you might not need them every trip, but if you run out while underwater, you won't care how beautiful the fish are. In trading, running out of capital means the game's over—no matter how good your next setup looks.

Chapter 7: Strategy Optimization

So, your strategy works... but could it work better? Time to fine-tune like a race car engineer—except instead of turbochargers, we're talking parameter tuning, machine learning, and just a pinch of statistical black magic. Be careful: if it's too perfect, you probably broke something.

This chapter guides readers through the process of refining algorithmic strategies. Topics include parameter optimization techniques like grid search, advanced methods such as genetic algorithms, and applying machine learning to trading. It also stresses the importance of preventing overfitting and maintaining realistic performance through careful feature selection and out-of-sample testing.

7.1 Parameter Tuning and Grid Search

I'll admit it: when I first started tuning strategy parameters, I felt like a mad scientist mixing potions. A little higher moving average length here, a tighter stop-loss there—until the backtest looked like a perfect money-printing machine. Then I took it live... and it performed about as well as a chocolate teapot. That was my introduction to why parameter tuning needs method, not magic.

What Is Parameter Tuning?

Definition:

Parameter tuning is the process of adjusting the input variables of your trading strategy (things like lookback periods, stop distances, or entry thresholds) to improve performance.

Why It Matters:

- Optimized parameters can significantly improve profitability.
- Helps adapt your system to current market conditions.
- Reduces trial-and-error guessing.

The Problem with Random Tinkering

Randomly changing settings until a backtest looks good is called curve fitting—and it's a fast track to strategies that fail in live markets. Curve fitting optimizes for past noise, not future performance.

Enter Grid Search

Definition:

Grid search is a systematic way to test multiple parameter combinations over a defined range to find the best-performing set.

How It Works:

1. Define parameters to optimize (e.g., moving average lengths, stop-loss %, take-profit %).
2. Set a range and step size for each.
3. Test every possible combination.
4. Rank results by performance metrics (e.g., Sharpe ratio, net profit, drawdown).

Example:

You're tuning a moving average crossover system with:

- Short MA length: 5, 10, 15
- Long MA length: 50, 100, 150

Grid search will test all 3 × 3 = 9 combinations systematically instead of guessing.

Advantages of Grid Search

- **Comprehensive:** Tests every combination in the defined range.
- **Reproducible:** Results are repeatable, not based on chance.
- **Easy to Understand:** Straightforward logic for both beginners and pros.

Drawbacks

- **Computationally Expensive:** Large parameter ranges can explode into thousands of tests.
- **Risk of Overfitting:** Even with systematic testing, the "best" set might just be lucky in historical data.

Avoiding the Overfitting Trap

Use Out-of-Sample Testing:

Split data into in-sample (for tuning) and out-of-sample (for validation).

Favor Simpler Models:

More parameters = more ways to overfit.

Look for Stable Regions:

If performance is strong across a range of settings, it's likely more robust than a single peak.

Cross-Validate:

Test across different time periods or market regimes.

My Approach

I use grid search as a first pass to identify promising parameter regions, not to lock in one "magic" set. Once I find a cluster of good results, I pick conservative settings that aren't sitting right at the top of the curve. Then I stress test them with walk-forward analysis.

Closing Thought

Think of parameter tuning like seasoning food—you want enough spice to make it tasty, but dump in the whole jar and you'll ruin the meal. In trading, a little optimization goes a long way; too much, and you're just feeding the backtest gods.

7.2 Genetic Algorithms and Machine Learning

When I first heard the term genetic algorithm, I thought, "Great, now I need a biology degree to trade." Luckily, no test tubes are required—just a computer and some patience. And machine learning? Let's just say the first time I tried it, I was so excited to see my model's 99% accuracy... until I realized it had "learned" that the market always goes up in my backtest period. Genius, but also useless.

What Are Genetic Algorithms (GAs)?

Definition:

Genetic algorithms are optimization techniques inspired by natural selection. They "evolve" solutions over time by keeping the best performers, mixing them together, and introducing small random changes—just like survival of the fittest in nature.

Why Use Them in Trading?

- Can search huge parameter spaces more efficiently than brute-force grid search.
- May find unexpected parameter combinations that still perform well.
- Handles nonlinear problems where standard optimization struggles.

How It Works in Practice:

1. **Initialize:** Generate a population of random parameter sets.
2. **Evaluate:** Test each set on your backtest.
3. **Select:** Keep the best-performing "individuals."

4. **Crossover:** Combine two good sets to make a new one.
5. **Mutate:** Randomly tweak parameters to explore new possibilities.
6. **Repeat:** Keep iterating until performance plateaus.

What About Machine Learning (ML)?

Definition:

Machine learning is about training algorithms to identify patterns in data and make predictions without being explicitly told the rules.

Common ML Approaches in Trading:

- **Supervised Learning:** Train a model with labeled data (e.g., historical price movement labeled as "up" or "down").

- **Unsupervised Learning:** Let the algorithm find patterns or clusters in unlabeled data (e.g., grouping similar market regimes).

- **Reinforcement Learning:** Teach an agent to take actions in a simulated market environment to maximize rewards over time.

Popular Tools/Libraries:

- **Python:** scikit-learn, XGBoost, TensorFlow, PyTorch

- **Languages:** Mostly Python, sometimes R or C++ for speed

GA vs. ML in Trading

Feature	Genetic Algorithms	Machine Learning
Goal	Find optimal parameters/settings	Learn patterns and predict outcomes
Strength	Efficient in big search spaces	Can handle complex, nonlinear relationships
Weakness	Can overfit if over-optimized	Needs lots of quality data
Typical Use	Optimize an existing strategy	Create predictive or adaptive strategies

Avoiding the Pitfalls

For GAs:

- Don't let them evolve for too many generations without constraints—they'll overfit to historical noise.
- Use multiple fitness metrics, not just profit.

For ML:

- Beware of data snooping—train/test splits are sacred.
- Focus on generalization, not perfection in training.
- Monitor live performance—models can "drift" as market behavior changes.

My Approach

I like to use genetic algorithms for parameter discovery and machine learning for pattern recognition. For example, I might evolve the best stop-loss/take-profit pairs with a GA, then feed those results into a machine learning model that decides whether to take trades based on market context.

Closing Thought

If grid search is like checking every drawer in your house to find your keys, genetic algorithms are like training a dog to sniff them out—and machine learning is like teaching the dog to also tell you if it's a good day to drive. In the wrong hands, they can be flashy but useless; in the right hands, they can make you a trading wizard.

7.3 Avoiding Overfitting and Curve Fitting

I once built a trading strategy so perfect it was almost suspicious. Every trade a winner. Every entry perfectly timed. It made more money on paper than Warren Buffett on his birthday. Then I took it live... and it promptly behaved like a toddler on a sugar crash. That was the day I truly understood the dark art of overfitting.

What Overfitting Really Means

Overfitting is what happens when your strategy learns the past so well it becomes useless for the future. You're not teaching it the market's habits—you're teaching it trivia about a specific point in time. It's like studying for a history test by memorizing one year's events, then being shocked when the teacher asks about the rest of the century.

Curve Fitting: The Special Subspecies

Curve fitting is a form of overfitting where you tweak parameters until the equity curve looks flawless. You keep adjusting the moving average length, stop-loss, or entry trigger until your backtest fits historical data like a glove. Problem is... the glove is made for one hand only, and the live market is wearing a different one entirely.

Why This Will Wreck You

- **Illusion of Skill:** The numbers say you're a genius. Reality says otherwise.

- **Poor Adaptability:** The market changes, and your "perfect" system can't handle it.

- **Capital Erosion:** You bleed cash faster than you can say "but the backtest looked amazing!"

Common Ways Traders Accidentally Overfit

Using Too Many Parameters

- The more variables you tweak, the more likely you're fitting noise.

Optimizing for Every Tick

- If you keep adjusting until there's no losing trade in the backtest, you've gone too far.

Ignoring Out-of-Sample Testing

- Without fresh data to validate on, you're just guessing.

Working With Too Little Data

- A hundred trades isn't enough to "prove" a strategy.

How to Keep Your Strategy Honest

1. Split the Data

- **In-Sample:** Data used for building and tuning.
- **Out-of-Sample:** Data used only for validation.
- **If it fails in the out**-of-sample, back to the drawing board.

2. Keep It Simple

- If you need 12 adjustable parameters to make it profitable, the edge probably isn't real.

3. Look for Robustness, Not Perfection

- A good strategy performs reasonably well across a range of parameter values, not just one ultra-specific setting.

4. Stress Test Like a Sadist

- Add fake noise to price data.
- Double transaction costs.
- Simulate bad fills and slippage.
- If it still holds up, you've got something solid.

5. Have a Logical Reason for Every Rule

- "Because it made money in backtests" is not a reason.

My Process in a Nutshell

I stop optimizing before the equity curve looks flawless. I prefer a strategy that works "well enough" across multiple scenarios over one that wins everything in one historical dataset. In my experience, the ugly-but-consistent systems pay the bills better than the backtest beauty queens.

Closing Thought

Overfitting is like rehearsing a conversation in your head, word-for-word, only to have the other person say something completely unexpected. You can't predict the future by memorizing the past—you can only prepare for its patterns. The goal isn't to create a perfect backtest; it's to create a resilient strategy that survives the market's curveballs.

7.4 Feature Engineering for Signal Enhancement

I'll be honest—when I first heard the term feature engineering, I thought it was about making my trading platform look prettier. Turns out, it's about making my data smarter. And while "signal enhancement" sounds like something you'd buy from a late-night infomercial, in trading it's the difference between spotting a real market edge and just listening to static.

What Is Feature Engineering?

Feature engineering is the process of taking raw market data and transforming it into more informative inputs (features) for your trading model or strategy.

It's the art of saying:

- *"Sure, I can use the closing price... but what if I also knew how volatile the last hour was, or how far price is from the daily average, or whether volume suddenly spiked?"*

Done right, it turns noisy, hard-to-use data into clean signals your strategy can actually understand.

Why It Matters

- Raw data is messy. Price and volume alone don't always reveal clear patterns.

- Better inputs mean better outputs. If your features are weak, even the smartest model will struggle.

- Signals often hide in transformations. Some patterns are only visible after you reframe the data.

Common Types of Features in Trading

Price-Based Features

- **Moving averages** (simple, exponential, weighted)
- **Price momentum** (rate of change, percentage change)
- Bollinger Band position

Volume-Based Features

- Volume moving average
- Volume spikes compared to recent history
- On-Balance Volume (OBV)

Volatility Features

- Average True Range (ATR)
- Standard deviation of returns
- Historical volatility

Market Structure Features

- Support/resistance distance
- High-low range in a given period
- Breakout indicators

Derived Ratios and Spreads

- Price-to-moving-average ratio
- Spread between two correlated assets
- Relative strength index (RSI) value

The Golden Rules of Feature Engineering

Start Simple

- A few strong, relevant features beat a dozen random ones.

Avoid Data Leakage

- Don't use future information in your features. For example, don't calculate tomorrow's average price for today's signal.

Test Incremental Value

- Add one feature at a time and check if it actually improves performance.

Normalize When Needed

- Many models perform better when features are scaled or standardized.

Keep It Interpretable

- Fancy features are useless if you can't explain what they represent.

My Go-To Process

- **Explore the Data** – I start by plotting and analyzing basic price and volume data to see what jumps out.

- **Brainstorm Candidate Features** – I think about what indicators or transformations might highlight patterns.

- **Build Iteratively** – I add features gradually, testing their predictive power one by one.

- **Prune Ruthlessly** – If a feature doesn't help, it goes. I don't keep dead weight in my models.

A Real-World Example

Say I'm building a short-term mean reversion strategy.

- Raw input: Price close, high, low, and volume.

Engineered features:

- Z-score of closing price relative to its 20-period moving average.
- Intraday volatility over the last 10 bars.
- Volume spike ratio (current volume ÷ average volume).

These engineered features help the model see when price is overextended, in a volatile environment, and on unusual trading activity—all useful for timing reversions.

Closing Thought

Feature engineering is like cooking: the ingredients (data) matter, but how you prepare them makes all the difference. Anyone can throw raw price data into a model, but if you season it with the right transformations, you can turn a bland dataset into a Michelin-star trading signal. Just remember—don't over-spice it, or you'll end up with a mess that tastes great in backtests and terrible in reality.

7.5 In-Sample vs Out-of-Sample Performance

Back when I was new to algorithmic trading, I thought a 300% return in backtesting meant I was ready to quit my job and start naming my yachts. Then my strategy went live, and instead of making a fortune, it made a slow, painful donation to the market. The problem? I'd only tested in-sample. It was like training for a marathon by running circles in my living room.

What Is In-Sample Data?

In-sample data is the portion of historical market data you use to build and optimize your strategy. This is where you tweak parameters, test ideas, and try to find that sweet spot.

Think of it like studying with the answer key—you're bound to look smart because you're learning from the exact questions you'll be tested on.

What Is Out-of-Sample Data?

Out-of-sample data is a separate chunk of historical data your strategy has never seen before. This is the real exam. If your system does well here, there's a better chance it will survive in live trading.

In other words, it's the "blind taste test" for your strategy—you find out if the recipe actually works when the market serves you something unexpected.

Why the Difference Matters

If your strategy only works on in-sample data, you've basically taught it to memorize the past instead of learning patterns. It's the same trap as overfitting—your model becomes a trivia champion in one specific historical period but fails in any other.

The Typical Workflow

Split the Data

- For example: 70% in-sample, 30% out-of-sample.
- The split should be chronological to preserve the sequence of market events.

Build and Optimize on In-Sample

- Adjust parameters and logic until you get decent performance—not perfection.

Validate on Out-of-Sample

- Run the strategy without any changes on the out-of-sample data.

Compare the Two

- If performance is similar, you might have a robust strategy.
- If out-of-sample performance collapses, back to the drawing board.

Common Pitfalls

Peeking at Out-of-Sample

- If you keep "just checking" the out-of-sample during development, you're contaminating it—it's no longer truly unseen.

Too Small Out-of-Sample Set

- If it's only a tiny fraction of the data, random luck could explain the results.

Using Different Market Conditions

- Out-of-sample should ideally cover different volatility regimes and market trends to test adaptability.

How I Use It

I treat in-sample like the practice field and out-of-sample like the actual match. If my strategy barely survives practice, it's not ready for game day. And if it crushes practice but flops in the game? That tells me I've built a strategy that's great at memorizing drills but hopeless in real play.

Closing Thought

Testing only in-sample is like rehearsing a speech in front of your dog and assuming the crowd will love it. Out-of-sample is where the polite head-nods end and the market gives you the real feedback—sometimes in the form of a punch to the wallet. The traders who survive long-term are the ones who embrace that reality check early.

Chapter 8: Execution and Live Deployment

You've coded it, tested it, and maybe even given it a cool name. Now it's showtime. But just as you're popping champagne, your internet drops, your broker API panics, and the bot thinks "flat" means "YOLO long." Welcome to live deployment, where reality checks are free and frequent.

In this chapter, readers learn how to transition strategies from development to live execution. It covers building a reliable execution engine, handling real-time data, managing technical failures, and distinguishing between paper trading and live trading. Additionally, the importance of system monitoring, error logging, and maintaining production-grade infrastructure is thoroughly explored.

8.1 Building an Execution Engine

When I first built my "execution engine," it was really just a glorified script that sent orders... sometimes. Other times it decided to take the day off, which was awkward when money was on the line. That's when I learned: an execution engine is not just a "send order" button — it's the heart and nervous system of your algorithmic trading operation. Get it wrong, and your strategy is just an expensive Excel file with dreams.

What Is an Execution Engine?

An execution engine is the software layer that turns trading decisions into actual market orders, monitors them, and makes sure they're handled efficiently.

It's the bridge between your strategy's ideas and the market's reality.

Think of it as the pit crew in Formula 1. Your trading model is the driver, but without a reliable crew, that car's not finishing the race.

The Core Responsibilities

Order Placement

- Send orders quickly and accurately.
- Handle multiple order types (market, limit, stop, etc.).

Order Management

- Track pending orders.
- Modify or cancel orders when needed.

Execution Quality Control

- Monitor fills, partial fills, and slippage.

- Log execution times and errors for later analysis.

Risk Checks

- Validate position sizes before sending orders.
- Prevent trades that exceed risk limits.

Connectivity and Failover

- Handle API disconnections gracefully.
- Failover to backup systems if needed.

Key Design Considerations

1. Latency Sensitivity

If you're doing high-frequency trading, every millisecond counts. For slower systems, latency is less critical but still worth minimizing.

2. Error Handling

APIs fail. Networks drop. The market changes between the time you send and the time you fill. Build robust exception handling so your bot doesn't panic.

3. Scalability

Your first version might handle 10 trades a day, but what if you need 10,000 in the future? Design for growth.

4. Logging and Monitoring

Keep detailed records of every order, execution time, slippage, and error. You'll thank yourself during debugging.

Components You'll Probably Need

- **Order Router** – Decides where and how to send an order.

- **Execution Algorithms** – Logic for how to slice large trades (e.g., TWAP, VWAP).
- **Risk Module** – Blocks trades that violate exposure limits.
- **API Interface** – Communicates with broker or exchange.
- **Failover Mechanisms** – Backup routing in case of outages.

My Personal Development Approach

Start with Paper Trading

- Hook the engine to a broker's sandbox environment to iron out basic order flow.

Move to Small Live Orders

- Test in real conditions with tiny size. Markets behave differently when you're actually sending orders.

Add Execution Optimizations

- Introduce logic for order slicing, timing, and venue selection to reduce slippage.

Stress Test

- Simulate network drops, bad fills, delayed confirmations. The goal is to break it in testing so it doesn't break in production.

Example Execution Flow

- **Signal Triggered:** Strategy says "Buy 100 shares of XYZ at market."
- **Risk Check:** Position size is okay, margin requirements met.
- **Order Sent:** API call to broker.

- **Acknowledgment:** Broker confirms receipt.
- **Fill Monitoring:** Engine tracks partial fills until complete or timeout.
- **Post-Trade Logging:** Record price, timestamp, and slippage.

Common Mistakes to Avoid

- **No Fail-Safes:** If the market moves against you mid-fill, you could end up with double positions.
- **Ignoring Partial Fills:** Some assets won't fill at once; handle them gracefully.
- **Overcomplicating Too Soon:** Keep version one simple, then iterate.

Closing Thought

Building an execution engine is a bit like installing plumbing. When it works, you barely think about it. When it fails, everything floods and you're suddenly very aware of how important it is. Get the foundation right, and your strategy can focus on making money instead of babysitting orders.

8.2 Real-Time Data Processing

The first time I set up a real-time data feed, I imagined I'd have this beautiful live dashboard with prices dancing gracefully like ballerinas. Instead, my screen started spitting out numbers so fast it looked like the Matrix, and my poor little script had a nervous breakdown. That's when I realized: real-time data processing is less about "watching prices" and more about managing chaos at high speed.

What Is Real-Time Data Processing?

In simple terms, it's the continuous collection, cleaning, and analysis of market data as it's generated — milliseconds after it happens.

For algorithmic trading, this is the lifeblood. Your strategy can't act on yesterday's news when you're competing with traders who act on yesterday's microsecond.

Types of Real-Time Data You'll Handle

Price Ticks

- Every trade that happens on the exchange.

Quotes

- Bid and ask prices plus sizes (Level I).
- Full order book snapshots and updates (Level II).

Market Depth

- Number of buy/sell orders at different price levels.

News and Events

- Earnings releases, economic reports, and even breaking tweets.

Derived Metrics

- Moving averages, volatility measures, or custom indicators calculated on the fly.

Challenges in Real-Time Data Processing

1. Latency

Data takes time to travel. Even microseconds matter in high-frequency trading.

2. Data Quality

Bad ticks, missing fields, or inconsistent timestamps can throw your strategy off course.

3. Throughput

You might receive thousands of updates per second — your system needs to keep up without choking.

4. Synchronization

When you have multiple data sources, aligning timestamps is critical.

My Approach to Building a Solid Real-Time Pipeline

Data Ingestion Layer

- Use broker/exchange APIs or dedicated market data providers.
- Ensure redundancy: a backup feed is your friend.

Normalization

- Convert all prices, timestamps, and symbols into a standard format.
- Handle different time zones, currency formats, and tick sizes.

Filtering & Cleaning

- Remove bad ticks.
- Fill small gaps if necessary.

Feature Calculation

- Calculate rolling averages, volatility, or other features your strategy needs.
- Keep it efficient — avoid heavy computations on every tick.

Event Handling

- Trigger strategy logic when specific conditions are met.

Tools & Technologies I've Used

- **Message Queues:** Kafka, RabbitMQ, or ZeroMQ for high-throughput data pipelines.
- **In-Memory Databases:** Redis or Memcached for lightning-fast lookups.
- **Stream Processing Frameworks:** Apache Flink, Spark Streaming for complex event processing.
- **Lightweight Python Options:** AsyncIO, websockets, and pandas for smaller-scale strategies.

Performance Tips from Experience

- **Batch Where Possible:** Process small chunks instead of every tick individually if your strategy allows.
- **Precompute Indicators:** Update rolling stats incrementally instead of recalculating from scratch.

- **Monitor Lag:** Continuously check if your data processing is falling behind the live feed.

- **Test Under Load:** Simulate peak trading days so your pipeline doesn't collapse when volatility spikes.

Common Mistakes to Avoid

- **Ignoring Timestamps:** You'll end up using stale data without realizing it.

- **Underestimating Data Volume:** A "small" feed can balloon in size during volatile markets.

- **Mixing Historical and Live Data Without Care:** It's easy to accidentally feed your live strategy a chunk of old history — and it won't thank you for it.

Closing Thought

Real-time data processing isn't glamorous. It's like being an air traffic controller for thousands of incoming flights — the job is invisible when done well, but if you miss one update, things can go south fast. Build it to be fast, clean, and reliable, and your strategy will actually get to make decisions in the same market everyone else is trading in — not the one from three seconds ago.

8.3 Dealing with Network and Infrastructure Failures

The first time my trading bot went down mid-session, I didn't notice right away. I was happily sipping coffee, thinking it was executing trades like a champ. In reality, it had been sitting frozen for twenty minutes, staring blankly into the void like a teenager in math class. That's when I learned: in algorithmic trading, Murphy's Law is always lurking in the server room.

Why Failures Are Inevitable

It doesn't matter how bulletproof you think your setup is — the market will find the one weak spot. Cables go bad. Routers reboot. Cloud servers mysteriously vanish for "scheduled maintenance" you didn't schedule. And sometimes your broker's API just decides to ghost you.

If your trading infrastructure is mission-critical (and it is), you need to assume things will break, and plan for the breakage before you ever hit "go live."

Common Points of Failure

Internet Connectivity

- Local ISP issues.
- Data center network drops.

Broker or Exchange API Outages

- Temporary downtime.
- Sudden rate limit enforcement.

Hardware Failures

- Overheating CPUs.

- Disk crashes.
- Power outages.

Software Crashes

- Memory leaks.
- Infinite loops.
- Unexpected API responses.

Cloud Provider Problems

- Region outages.
- Latency spikes.

My Core Strategies for Staying Online

1. Redundancy Everywhere

If one ISP goes down, have another ready.

If one server fails, another should take over without you lifting a finger.

2. Heartbeat Monitoring

Your systems should send "I'm alive" pings every few seconds. If one stops, the backup should step in immediately.

3. Failover Logic in Code

If your main data feed fails, switch to the backup feed automatically. Same for execution APIs.

4. Local vs. Remote Hosting

I run critical components in colocation data centers close to exchange servers to reduce latency — but I still keep a local copy running in case my primary site goes dark.

5. Graceful Shutdown Procedures

If everything is failing at once, have a safe mode: cancel all open orders, flatten positions, and stop trading until manual inspection.

Example Failure Scenario & Recovery Plan

Scenario: Main execution server loses internet.

Response Plan:

- Heartbeat monitor detects downtime in 2 seconds.
- Backup server in another data center takes over execution duties.
- Primary server automatically cancels stale orders once reconnected.
- Logs all events for postmortem review.

Tools & Techniques I've Found Useful

- **Pingdom / UptimeRobot** – External uptime monitoring.
- **Prometheus + Grafana** – Real-time metrics and alerts.
- **HAProxy / Load Balancers** – Distribute load and failover automatically.
- **UPS (Uninterruptible Power Supply)** – Buy time during short outages.
- **Docker & Kubernetes** – Fast redeployment of crashed containers.

Testing Your Disaster Plan

Most people write a failover plan and never test it. That's like having a parachute you've never opened before.

- **Simulate Failures** – Unplug network cables, kill processes, take servers offline.

- **Measure Recovery Time** – How fast does the backup kick in?

- **Check Trade Safety** – Are orders canceled or safely passed to the backup engine?

Common Mistakes to Avoid

- **Single Points of Failure** – Even one can take your whole operation down.

- **Overcomplicating Failover Logic** – Keep it simple; complex systems fail in complex ways.

- **Assuming the Broker Will Protect You** – They have their own problems to deal with.

Closing Thought

Trading systems don't die from one big failure; they die from a hundred tiny ones you didn't prepare for. Build like you're expecting disaster at any moment, and you'll be pleasantly surprised when you survive it. Remember: in this business, "paranoid" is just another word for "still trading tomorrow."

8.4 Paper Trading vs. Live Trading

When I first tried paper trading, I felt like a Wall Street genius. My "trades" were nailing tops and bottoms, profits were rolling in, and I started daydreaming about yachts. Then I switched to live trading... and the market promptly smacked me so hard I started checking if my strategy had developed a personal vendetta against me.

That's the moment every algo trader learns: paper trading and live trading are the same game in theory, but in practice they're about as similar as playing chess against a computer and playing chess while someone throws water balloons at you.

What Is Paper Trading?

Paper trading is trading without risking real money — using a simulated environment that mirrors live market conditions as closely as possible. Historically, people literally wrote trades down on paper to track hypothetical outcomes. Today, it's usually done on broker-provided simulators or custom backtesting environments running in "live" mode with market data feeds.

Why Paper Trading Is Valuable

Low-Risk Learning

- You can test execution logic without losing your shirt.

Debugging Your Code

- Catch silly bugs before they cost you real money.

Broker API Familiarity

- Learn the quirks of order submissions, modifications, and cancellations.

Strategy Validation in Real Time

- See how your system behaves in current market conditions.

The Limitations of Paper Trading

Here's the part they don't tell you in the marketing brochure:

No Real Slippage

- Simulators fill orders instantly at mid-price unless programmed otherwise.

No Psychological Pressure

- It's easy to hold a losing trade in a simulator when there's no pain involved.

Unrealistic Liquidity

- Paper accounts often let you "fill" huge orders that would never execute at that size in the real market.

Latency Illusion

- Simulators rarely replicate the tiny (but deadly) delays in real order execution.

Making Paper Trading More Realistic

If you want paper trading to be useful, you've got to rough it up a bit:

- **Simulate Slippage** – Add a few ticks of delay and unfavorable price movement to market orders.

- **Respect Liquidity** – Only "fill" orders if they'd realistically match in the order book.

- **Include Fees & Commissions** – A strategy that works before fees can implode after them.

- **Track Realistic Position Sizes** – Don't paper trade with fantasy capital you'll never have.

Transitioning from Paper to Live

This is where traders either become legends or cautionary tales.

My Steps for a Smooth Transition:

- **Go Small** – Start with the smallest live position sizes possible.

- **Shadow Trading** – Run paper and live in parallel for a few weeks to compare.

- **Expect Differences** – Account for slippage, missed fills, and extra volatility.

- **Refine, Then Scale** – Only increase size when live results match expectations.

Common Mistakes I See

- Treating paper trading as proof of profitability.

- Ignoring the emotional difference when real money is at stake.

- Jumping from paper to full-size live trading overnight.

Closing Thought

Paper trading is like flight simulation. It teaches you the controls, helps you practice emergency procedures, and lets you crash without consequence. But no simulator can prepare you for the first time you hit turbulence with your money on the line. Respect the gap, train smart, and remember: paper profits spend a lot worse than the real kind.

8.5 Monitoring and Logging for Production

When you first launch an algo into live trading, you feel like a proud parent watching their kid walk into school on the first day. You've built it, tested it, debugged it... and now you just hope it doesn't get into trouble. But here's the truth: if you're not monitoring and logging everything it does, you're basically sending it into a mosh pit without earplugs.

Why Monitoring Matters

In production, your algorithm is no longer just code — it's a living, breathing money machine. If it goes rogue, it can drain your account before you've finished making a sandwich. Monitoring is your early warning system.

- **Catch Failures Early** – From network drops to stuck orders.
- **Spot Performance Drift** – When a strategy suddenly starts performing differently than in testing.
- **Meet Compliance Needs** – Some jurisdictions require you to keep trade records.

What to Monitor

System Health

- CPU, RAM, and disk usage
- Network connectivity and latency
- Heartbeat checks for key processes

Market Data Feeds

- Are ticks coming in on time?

- Is there an unusual gap in quotes?

Execution Layer

- Order submission success/failure rates
- Fill times and slippage metrics
- Rejected or canceled orders

Strategy Performance

- Current P/L
- Open positions
- Risk exposure vs. limits

Why Logging Is Your Best Friend

Logs are like a black box recorder for your trading system — when something goes wrong, they tell the story. Without logs, you're just guessing.

Good Logging Practices:

- **Timestamp Everything** – To the millisecond if possible.
- **Separate Levels** – Info, Warning, Error, Critical.
- **Log Inputs and Outputs** – Market data received, orders sent, execution reports.
- **Include Context** – Which strategy, which symbol, what conditions triggered the action.

Tools I've Found Useful

- **Prometheus + Grafana** – Real-time metrics and alerting.

- **ELK Stack (Elasticsearch, Logstash, Kibana)** – Searchable, structured logs.
- **Papertrail / Loggly** – Cloud-based log aggregation.
- **PagerDuty / Opsgenie** – Wake-you-up alerts for critical events.

The Art of Alerting

A common rookie mistake is setting too many alerts. The first week you'll be responding to every ping like a firefighter; by week three you'll be ignoring them all.

- **Alert on Actionable Events Only** – Not just "interesting" metrics.
- **Set Severity Levels** – Red for stop-trading-now, yellow for check-when-you-can.
- **Throttle Repeat Alerts** – Don't send 500 notifications for the same problem.

My "Oh No" Story

Once, a typo in my order routing code started sending duplicate orders. My logs showed "Order sent" twice for every trade, but I didn't have an alert on unusual order volume. I only noticed when my margin warning came in — which was about as welcome as a chainsaw in a yoga class.

Closing Thought

Monitoring and logging aren't the exciting parts of algo trading. Nobody brags at parties about their perfectly formatted log files. But when things go sideways — and they will — your logs will be the only thing standing between you and a very expensive guessing game. Think of it as the security camera footage for your money.

Chapter 9: Advanced Strategies and Quant Techniques

Now that you're past the baby-bot phase, it's time to suit up for the big leagues. Think statistical arbitrage, machine learning models that almost scare you, and trades that happen faster than a sneeze. Welcome to the quantum realm of finance.

This chapter introduces more sophisticated algorithmic approaches, including statistical arbitrage, machine learning-driven strategies, and high-frequency trading techniques. It also explores emerging areas such as sentiment analysis using alternative data and constructing multi-asset, cross-market strategies. The chapter provides a glimpse into the cutting edge of quantitative finance and its tools.

9.1 Statistical Arbitrage and Pairs Trading

When I first heard "statistical arbitrage," I thought it was some kind of secret Wall Street magic trick — like pulling a rabbit out of a regression model. In reality, it's less about pulling rabbits and more about pulling tiny, consistent profits from patterns that most traders overlook. And pairs trading? That's the gateway drug.

What Is Statistical Arbitrage?

Statistical arbitrage (stat arb, for short) is a market-neutral trading approach that uses statistical and mathematical models to exploit pricing inefficiencies between securities. You're not betting on the market going up or down — you're betting on relationships between instruments returning to their "normal" state.

Think of it as playing matchmaker between two stocks, futures contracts, or ETFs that normally dance together. If one starts moonwalking while the other is still doing the cha-cha, you bet they'll eventually get back in sync.

Enter Pairs Trading

Pairs trading is the simplest and most famous form of statistical arbitrage. You identify two historically correlated assets — say, Coca-Cola (KO) and Pepsi (PEP). When the price spread between them widens beyond a certain statistical threshold, you:

- Buy the underperformer
- Short the outperformer

When the spread narrows back to the historical mean, you close both positions and pocket the difference.

Why It Works

Mean Reversion

- The relationship between the two assets tends to revert to its historical average.

Market Neutrality

Gains from one side can offset losses on the other, reducing exposure to overall market moves.

Statistical Edge

- You're not guessing direction — you're trading based on a quantifiable relationship.

The Basic Workflow

Select Candidate Pairs

- Look for assets in the same sector or with economic links.

Check Historical Correlation

- Pearson correlation > 0.8 is a common starting point.

Test for Cointegration

- This is more robust than correlation — cointegration means the spread between the assets is stable over time.

Calculate the Spread

- Spread = Price of Asset A – β × Price of Asset B (β from regression).

Define Entry/Exit Signals

- Example: Enter when spread > $+2\sigma$ or < -2σ; exit when spread reverts to the mean.

Backtest and Optimize

- Avoid the temptation to overfit thresholds to historical data.

Risks and Pitfalls

Relationship Breakdown

- Just because two stocks moved together in the past doesn't mean they'll keep dancing.

Short Squeeze Risk

- If your short leg gets squeezed, market neutrality won't save you.

Execution Costs

- You're trading two legs for every trade — commissions and slippage can eat your edge.

Overfitting Models

- Making a spread rule that worked perfectly on the past but flops in the future.

Tools I Use for Stat Arb

- **Python Libraries:** statsmodels (cointegration tests), pandas (data handling), numpy (math)

- **Visualization:** Plotting spread and Z-score over time to eyeball entry/exit points.

- **Backtesting:** Custom frameworks or libraries like backtrader.

My "Learning the Hard Way" Story

Early in my career, I ran a pairs trade on two tech stocks that had been inseparable for years. Then one of them announced a surprise acquisition that completely changed its business model. The spread blew out and never reverted. I learned two things:

1. Cointegration is not a lifetime guarantee.
2. Reading the news occasionally won't kill you.

Closing Thought

Statistical arbitrage and pairs trading can be the clean, clinical side of trading — more math than gut feel, more statistics than CNBC headlines. But like any romance, just because two assets have history doesn't mean they're destined for the future. Keep your models sharp, your stop-losses tighter, and your eyes open for that one dance partner who's about to change the music.

9.2 Machine Learning in Strategy Design

When I first dipped my toes into machine learning (ML) for trading, I half expected my computer to morph into some kind of stock market oracle, whispering the next big winner into my ear. Spoiler: it didn't. What it did do was give me a powerful toolbox for extracting subtle patterns from mountains of market data — patterns that a plain-old moving average could never dream of spotting.

Why Use Machine Learning in Trading?

Machine learning thrives when the relationship between variables is too complex for simple rules. Markets are messy, noisy, and non-linear — and ML is particularly good at making sense of that chaos, at least enough to find a probabilistic edge.

You can use ML to:

- Classify market regimes (bull, bear, sideways)
- Predict short-term price direction or volatility
- Optimize position sizing dynamically
- Detect anomalies or outliers in market data

Key Machine Learning Approaches in Trading

Supervised Learning

- **You feed the model historical inputs** (features) and known outcomes (labels).
- **Example:** Predicting whether tomorrow's return will be positive or negative.

- **Algorithms:** Logistic Regression, Random Forests, Gradient Boosted Trees, Neural Networks.

Unsupervised Learning

- **No labels** — just finding structure in data.

- **Example:** Clustering assets into groups with similar behavior to diversify risk.

- **Algorithms:** K-means, Hierarchical Clustering, PCA for dimensionality reduction.

Reinforcement Learning

- The model learns by trial and error, receiving rewards for profitable actions.

- Example: An agent deciding when to buy, hold, or sell based on continuous feedback from the market.

The Workflow for ML Strategy Design

Define the Objective

- Don't just say "make money." Be specific: maximize Sharpe ratio, reduce drawdowns, predict volatility spikes, etc.

Data Collection

- Historical price data, fundamental data, sentiment data, alternative datasets (satellite imagery, credit card spend, etc.).

Feature Engineering

- This is where you craft the inputs: moving averages, volatility measures, RSI, order book imbalances, macro indicators.

Model Selection

- Start simple, then get fancy. Often, a well-tuned gradient boosting model beats an overcomplicated neural net.

Training and Validation

- Split data into training, validation, and test sets.
- Use cross-validation to prevent overfitting.

Backtesting

- Apply the trained model's signals to historical data to simulate performance.

Deployment

- Integrate the model into your execution engine with live monitoring and fail-safes.

Common Pitfalls

Overfitting

- Your model fits history perfectly but fails in live trading.

Data Snooping Bias

- Testing too many features and cherry-picking the best results.

Lookahead Bias

- Accidentally giving your model information it wouldn't have at decision time.

Changing Market Regimes

- A model trained in a bull market may fail miserably in a sideways or bear market.

Tools I've Found Useful

- **Python Libraries:** scikit-learn, xgboost, lightgbm, tensorflow, pytorch
- **Data Processing:** pandas, numpy, dask
- **Visualization:** matplotlib, seaborn, plotly
- **Experiment Tracking:** MLflow, Weights & Biases

A Quick "Humbling Moment" Story

I once trained a neural network on five years of intraday stock data. The backtest looked amazing — 85% win rate, smooth equity curve, barely any drawdowns. I was ready to quit my day job. Then I went live... and the model lost money three days in a row. Turns out I'd accidentally leaked future data into my training set. The "perfect" model was just a perfect cheater.

Closing Thought

Machine learning isn't a magic bullet — it's a high-maintenance partner. It can uncover patterns you'd never find manually, but it can also lure you into false confidence if you're not careful with validation and testing. Use it as an amplifier for good trading ideas, not a replacement for sound market logic. Because in trading, the smartest algorithm in the room still loses money if it's overconfident and underprepared.

9.3 High-Frequency Trading Techniques

High-frequency trading (HFT) is where speed stops being a "nice to have" and becomes the entire business model. We're talking about strategies that live and die in microseconds. I remember my first conversation with an HFT guy — I asked him if he cared about fundamentals, and he looked at me like I'd just asked if he used astrology to time trades. In HFT, fundamentals are a quaint bedtime story.

What Exactly Is HFT?

HFT is the art (and science) of using ultra-fast computers, lightning-quick market data feeds, and hyper-optimized algorithms to execute a massive number of trades in fractions of a second. Profits are razor-thin per trade, but the volume makes it meaningful.

If normal trading is like playing chess, HFT is like playing 1,000 games of speed chess at the same time, where the pieces occasionally teleport.

Core Pillars of HFT

Latency Minimization

- Every nanosecond counts. Firms literally measure cable lengths to shave microseconds off transmission times.

- Techniques: Colocation (placing your servers in the same data center as the exchange), direct market access (DMA), microwave and laser data transmission between cities.

Market Microstructure Knowledge

- Understanding the rules, matching engine quirks, and order priority systems of each exchange.

- Sometimes, knowing how an exchange handles cancellations or partial fills is worth more than your model.

Execution Algorithms

- **Smart order routing:** deciding which venue to hit based on price, liquidity, and latency.

- **Order types:** iceberg orders, post-only, hidden liquidity hunting.

Real-Time Data Processing

- Processing Level II order book data in microseconds.

- Identifying shifts in supply and demand before the rest of the market reacts.

Common HFT Strategies

Market Making

- Continuously posting bids and offers to earn the spread. Requires lightning-fast risk management.

Statistical Arbitrage at Microsecond Scale

- Similar to pairs trading, but exploiting tiny price discrepancies across correlated instruments — and doing it before anyone else sees them.

Latency Arbitrage

- Capitalizing on delays between different market data feeds.

- Example: Spotting a price change in futures before it's reflected in the ETF.

Liquidity Detection

- Probing the market to find hidden orders and then trading around them.

Technology Stack

- **Languages:** C++ (still king for raw speed), Java, low-latency Python only for research
- **Networking:** Kernel bypass networking (e.g., Solarflare NICs), FPGA acceleration for order processing
- **Hardware:** Custom-built servers, ultra-low-latency switches, solid-state storage for logging
- **Monitoring:** Real-time telemetry dashboards — even a 10-millisecond hiccup can cost thousands

Risks Unique to HFT

Infrastructure Failures

- Your "strategy" might be perfect, but if your server freezes for 200ms, you're dead in the water.

Regulatory Scrutiny

- Certain HFT practices (like spoofing) are illegal and aggressively monitored.

Adverse Selection

- Getting picked off by someone faster when your quotes are stale.

Arms Race Costs

- The money spent on hardware, data feeds, and engineering talent can eat most of your edge if you're not in the top tier.

My "Learning Curve" Story

I once tried building a "lightweight" HFT strategy using Python. Backtest looked great. But in live testing, I learned that my Python script was slower than a grandma counting change at the grocery store. By the time my algorithm decided to act, the opportunity had evaporated. Lesson learned: in HFT, "good enough" speed is never good enough.

Closing Thought

HFT is like Formula 1 racing — thrilling, expensive, and brutally competitive. If you have the engineering skill, market microstructure expertise, and capital to play at that level, it can be a thing of beauty. But if you bring a bicycle to the racetrack, don't be surprised when you get lapped before you've even crossed the starting line.

9.4 Sentiment Analysis and Alternative Data

I'll be honest — when I first heard about traders scraping tweets to make trading decisions, I thought it was ridiculous. Fast forward a few years, and there I was, building a pipeline that parsed news headlines and Reddit posts faster than you can say "tendies." Turns out, markets aren't just about numbers; they're also about feelings — and if you can quantify those feelings before everyone else, you might just have an edge.

What Is Sentiment Analysis?

Sentiment analysis is the process of using algorithms to gauge the emotional tone of a piece of text (or speech, or even video). In trading, this typically means scoring news articles, tweets, earnings transcripts, or analyst reports as "positive," "negative," or "neutral" toward a stock, sector, or market.

If price data tells you what happened, sentiment data often hints at why it happened — or what might happen next.

Sources of Sentiment Data

News Feeds

- Bloomberg, Reuters, Dow Jones — professional sources with high-quality text.
- Great for capturing major events and market-moving headlines.

Social Media

- Twitter, Stocktwits, Reddit, TikTok (yes, really).
- Much noisier, but faster and sometimes predictive for retail-driven stocks.

Earnings Calls and Transcripts

- CEOs say a lot without saying much — tone analysis can reveal hidden confidence or caution.

Analyst Reports

- A shift in tone can foreshadow a change in recommendation.

Alternative Data — The Secret Sauce

Sentiment is just one piece of the alternative data puzzle. Alternative data refers to non-traditional information sources that can help you spot trends earlier than the competition. Examples include:

- **Satellite Imagery:** Tracking the number of cars in retail parking lots.
- **Credit Card Transactions:** Monitoring consumer spending patterns in near real-time.
- **Web Traffic:** Analyzing visitor trends to e-commerce or travel sites.
- **App Usage Data:** Tracking downloads, session length, or user growth.
- **Shipping & Trade Data:** Watching cargo movement patterns.

How to Process and Use Sentiment

Data Collection

- APIs like Twitter, GDELT (for global events), or premium data providers.

Preprocessing

- Remove stopwords, normalize text, handle misspellings and slang.

- Social media often requires special handling for emojis, sarcasm, and abbreviations.

Sentiment Scoring

- **Lexicon-based:** Use dictionaries of positive/negative words.

- **Machine Learning:** Train classifiers (Naive Bayes, SVM, Transformers like BERT).

Signal Generation

- Combine sentiment scores with market data to create predictive indicators.

- Example: Buy when sentiment spikes alongside high trading volume.

Example in Practice

Let's say Tesla's sentiment score jumps 30% in an hour due to a surprise product announcement. If you detect and act on that before the market fully prices it in, you might catch a fast-moving rally. On the flip side, if you see a flood of negative sentiment about a company's supply chain, it might be a heads-up to short before earnings disappointment.

Challenges and Pitfalls

- **Noise:** Not every tweet matters — sometimes people just like to yell into the void.

- **False Positives:** Sarcasm and irony can flip the sentiment score in the wrong direction.

- **Data Cost:** High-quality alternative data feeds can be expensive.

- **Changing Language:** Slang evolves fast, and models can become outdated.

Tools and Libraries

- **Python:** NLTK, TextBlob, VADER for lexicon methods; transformers for deep learning models.
- **Data Pipelines:** Apache Kafka, Airflow for streaming and scheduling.
- **Visualization:** plotly, matplotlib, word clouds for exploratory analysis.

My "Oops" Moment

I once fed a sentiment model unfiltered Reddit data to predict meme stock moves. The model immediately assigned every stock the highest possible bullish score. Why? Because the training set was 90% and "to the moon." Great for laughs, terrible for PnL. Lesson: clean your data, especially when your "analysts" are anonymous internet users with rocket emojis in their usernames

Closing Thought

Sentiment and alternative data aren't magic — but they can give you an edge when used alongside solid market analysis. The real trick is in separating the signal from the noise and acting faster than everyone else. Because in trading, knowing how the crowd feels can sometimes be more valuable than knowing the actual facts. After all, markets move on perception long before they move on reality.

9.5 Multi-Asset and Cross-Market Strategies

When I first started trading, I was like that kid who only eats one type of cereal every morning — for me, it was stocks, and nothing else. Futures? Bonds? FX? Commodities? Those were "someone else's thing." But then I realized that markets aren't isolated silos — they're a web of relationships. Miss those links, and you're basically reading one page of a mystery novel and trying to guess the plot twist.

Multi-asset and cross-market strategies are about trading across different asset classes and using the relationships between them to find opportunities that might be invisible if you focus on just one.

What Do We Mean by Multi-Asset?

Multi-asset simply means dealing with more than one type of financial instrument in your strategy. Instead of just equities, you might also trade:

- **Equities** (stocks, ETFs)
- **Fixed Income** (government and corporate bonds)
- **Commodities** (gold, oil, agricultural products)
- **Currencies** (FX spot, futures)
- **Cryptocurrencies** (Bitcoin, Ethereum, and friends)
- **Derivatives** (options, futures, swaps)

Cross-market strategies take this a step further — they don't just include multiple assets; they exploit relationships between them.

Examples of Cross-Market Relationships

Equity-Commodity Links

- Airlines' stock prices often move inversely to oil prices. If oil spikes, airline costs go up, margins shrink, and share prices may drop.

Currency-Equity Connections

- Export-heavy companies benefit when their home currency weakens — their goods become cheaper abroad.

Bond-Equity Dynamics

- In risk-off markets, money flows out of stocks and into bonds (yields drop). Reverse happens in risk-on environments.

Crypto-Traditional Market Links

- BTC sometimes trades like a high-beta tech stock, other times like a flight-to-safety asset — identifying the current regime can be an edge.

Strategy Archetypes

Statistical Arbitrage Across Assets

- Pair or basket trading with different asset classes that historically move together.

Lead-Lag Strategies

- One market reacts faster than another to the same information. Example: Interest rate futures moving before bank stocks after a Fed announcement.

Relative Value Across Geographies

- Trading S&P futures vs. Euro Stoxx futures when valuations or macro conditions diverge.

Hedged Multi-Asset Portfolios

- Long equities with a commodity or currency hedge to reduce drawdowns.

Data & Technology Needs

Synchronized Data Feeds

- You need accurate timestamps across all assets, otherwise your "lead-lag" signal turns into "lag-lag."

Cross-Market Analytics

- Tools for correlation, cointegration, and regime detection.

Execution Infrastructure

- Access to multiple exchanges and brokers; smart order routing across asset classes.

Risks in Multi-Asset Strategies

Correlation Breakdown

- Just because two assets have been linked historically doesn't mean they always will be.

Execution Complexity

- More markets means more moving parts — and more chances for something to fail.

Capital Allocation Challenges

- Deciding how much risk to assign to each market.

Regulatory Overlap

- Different asset classes often fall under different regulators, rules, and reporting requirements.

My "It Looked Perfect in Backtest" Moment

I once built a lead-lag model between crude oil and the Canadian dollar. The backtest showed a gorgeous, steady equity curve. In live trading? The correlation fell apart within a month because of a surprise change in Canadian fiscal policy. It was like expecting a perfect tango partner and getting someone who suddenly decided to breakdance mid-song. Moral: cross-asset relationships can be seasonal, regime-dependent, or just plain fickle.

Closing Thought

Multi-asset and cross-market strategies can give you diversification, unique edges, and more ways to express your market view. But they're not "set and forget" — relationships evolve, and you've got to keep testing your assumptions. If you can master the interplay between markets, you stop trading in one narrow lane and start driving the whole highway. Just... watch out for the oncoming traffic.

Chapter 10: Ethics, Regulations, and the Future

Just because your bot can flood the market with a thousand quotes doesn't mean it should. With great trading power comes great regulatory scrutiny—and a moral compass (hopefully). Plus, what happens when the bots start writing their own bots?

This final chapter addresses the ethical and regulatory dimensions of algorithmic trading. It provides an overview of key regulatory bodies like the SEC and MiFID, outlines compliance obligations, and discusses the importance of avoiding manipulative practices. The chapter concludes with a discussion on the role of AI in trading and potential future developments in the industry.

10.1 Regulatory Frameworks (SEC, MiFID, etc.)

Let's be honest: talking about regulations is like discussing your dentist's appointment — everyone knows it's important, nobody's excited about it, and if you ignore it too long, you'll regret it. In trading, that regret doesn't come as a toothache — it comes as a fine, a trading ban, or a call from a very serious-sounding person who addresses you by your full name.

The reality is that whether you're a one-person algo shop or a billion-dollar hedge fund, you can't just code strategies, hit "run," and hope the regulators don't notice you. They will notice. The key is knowing the rules of the playground you're trading in.

The Big Players in Regulation

1. SEC (Securities and Exchange Commission) – United States

- **Oversees securities markets:** stocks, ETFs, bonds.
- **Key focus:** investor protection, market integrity, and fair dealing.
- **If you're trading U.S. equities,** you're in SEC territory.
- **Major rules you'll bump into:**
- **Reg NMS (National Market System):** Ensures best execution and price transparency.
- **Reg SHO:** Governs short-selling rules.

2. CFTC (Commodity Futures Trading Commission) – United States

- Regulates futures, options on futures, and swaps.

- Oversees exchanges like CME and ICE.
- Algo traders here need to know about "disruptive trading practices" rules — no spoofing, layering, or other manipulative tricks.

3. FINRA (Financial Industry Regulatory Authority) – United States

- A self-regulatory organization that oversees broker-dealers.
- If your trades go through a broker, FINRA likely touches your life indirectly.

4. MiFID II (Markets in Financial Instruments Directive II) – European Union

- A sweeping set of rules governing EU markets.
- Heavy focus on transparency, investor protection, and reducing systemic risk.
- Algo traders must register their algorithms with venues, perform annual testing, and maintain detailed audit trails.

5. FCA (Financial Conduct Authority) – United Kingdom

- Regulates financial markets, firms, and traders in the UK.
- Known for strict algorithmic trading oversight, including pre-trade risk controls.

6. ASIC (Australian Securities and Investments Commission) – Australia

- Oversees financial services and markets in Australia.
- Increasing scrutiny on high-frequency and algorithmic strategies.

Key Regulatory Themes for Algo Traders

Registration & Authorization

- Some jurisdictions require you to register your algorithms or even yourself as a trader.

Audit Trails

- You must be able to show exactly what your algo did, when, and why.

Market Abuse Prevention

- Spoofing, layering, and "quote stuffing" can get you in serious trouble.

Risk Controls

- Kill switches, order throttling, and position limits are not optional — regulators expect them.

Testing & Certification

- Some regions require documented backtesting and stress testing before an algo goes live.

My "Brush with Compliance" Moment

Years ago, I was running a strategy on U.S. equities that relied on rapid order cancellations. Totally legal, right? Well, one day I got a friendly (read: terrifying) inquiry from my broker asking why my cancel-to-trade ratio was so high. I explained my logic, showed my code and logs, and it turned out fine — but I learned a key lesson: in the eyes of a regulator, intent matters less than impact. If your behavior looks manipulative, expect questions.

Staying on the Right Side of the Line

- **Know Your Jurisdiction** – Laws differ wildly across regions.

- **Keep Detailed Logs** – Store order history, market data snapshots, and decision logic.

- **Work with Compliance Early** – If you're in a firm, make friends with compliance officers. They can save you from yourself.

- **Automate Risk Checks** – Your algo should stop itself before it becomes a problem.

- **Stay Current** – Regulations evolve. What's fine today might be banned tomorrow.

Closing Thought

Regulations can feel like red tape slowing down your big money-making machine, but they also protect you from the market turning into a Wild West shootout. In the long run, playing by the rules isn't just about avoiding trouble — it's about building trust with brokers, counterparties, and even your own investors. Plus, if you're really clever, you can spot opportunities in how regulations change — new rules often shift liquidity, volatility, and even market structure.

And remember: "I didn't know the rule" is about as effective with regulators as "the dog ate my homework" was with your third-grade teacher.

10.2 Avoiding Market Manipulation Practices

When you first dive into algo trading, there's this intoxicating feeling: "I can make the market dance if I code it right." Then you realize — yes, you can make the market dance, but if it looks like you're forcing the choreography in a way regulators don't like, you'll be hauled off the floor before the music stops.

Market manipulation isn't just shady ethics — it's a fast track to fines, bans, and possibly explaining your "innovative strategy" to people wearing government badges. The tricky part? Some manipulative practices don't look obviously wrong at first.

Common Forms of Manipulation to Avoid

1. Spoofing

- Placing large orders with no intent to execute, just to nudge the market and then canceling them quickly.
- Famous cases have ended in multi-million-dollar penalties and prison time.

2. Layering

- Similar to spoofing, but done in multiple layers of orders at different price levels to fake depth in the order book.

3. Quote Stuffing

- Flooding the market with orders and cancellations to slow others down or create confusion.
- In today's low-latency world, regulators spot this faster than you can say "order rejected."

4. Wash Trading

- Buying and selling the same asset to create fake volume.
- Illegal in most regulated markets — but still crops up in unregulated crypto exchanges.

5. Marking the Close

- Trading aggressively at the market close to influence the closing price (and, conveniently, the valuation of your position).

6. Pump-and-Dump

- Artificially inflating a price with misleading orders or information, then selling into the spike.

The Algo Trader's Grey Zone

Here's where it gets messy: your perfectly legitimate market-making strategy could look like spoofing if you're constantly canceling and replacing quotes. I once ran a high-frequency equities strategy where my cancel-to-trade ratio exceeded 80%. Totally legal. Totally within my risk parameters. Still got a "We'd like to have a chat" email from the broker.

Lesson learned: intent matters in the law, but appearance matters in surveillance systems. If your pattern looks manipulative, expect scrutiny.

Best Practices to Stay Clean

Code With Intent in Mind

- Don't just think about P&L. Think about how your order patterns look to an exchange's surveillance team.

Throttle Your Order Activity

- Keep cancel-to-trade ratios reasonable unless your strategy requires high activity — and be ready to justify it.

Avoid Artificial Market Signals

- If your algo's only purpose is to provoke reactions without genuine trading intent, you're in the danger zone.

Log Everything

- Keep timestamped order logs and market data snapshots to prove your side if questioned.

Test in Simulation Before Live

- Some manipulative-looking patterns emerge unintentionally during early live runs — spot them before a regulator does.

Review Strategy Against Market Abuse Laws

- Especially if you operate in multiple jurisdictions — "acceptable" in one market might be "felony" in another.

My "Close Call" Story

I once had a futures strategy that placed a small set of probing orders to detect hidden liquidity. Worked beautifully — until one day it triggered an exchange inquiry because my orders consistently moved the displayed depth before being canceled. I explained it was part of a legitimate price discovery process, but that conversation taught me two things:

1. Regulators love asking "Why did you do that?"
2. If your answer is "Because it worked," you're in trouble.

Closing Thought

Avoiding market manipulation isn't just about steering clear of the obvious bad stuff — it's about being aware of how your strategies look through the eyes of surveillance algorithms and compliance officers. The safest way to stay out of trouble? Design strategies that would still make sense if every single order you placed was displayed on a big screen in a regulatory office.

And if you ever think, "I wonder if this would raise eyebrows?" — congratulations, your eyebrows just raised the compliance department's eyebrows.

10.3 Ethical Considerations in Algo Trading

The moment you give an algorithm the power to move real money, you've basically created a digital intern who works 24/7, never complains, and never asks for coffee breaks. But unlike human interns, this one won't hesitate to accidentally wreck the market in milliseconds if you give it the wrong instructions. Which means you — the human — have to be the moral compass.

Ethics in algo trading isn't just "don't break the law." You can follow the rules to the letter and still design something that causes real harm — to other traders, to market stability, even to your own investors. The question isn't just "Is it legal?" but "Is it right?"

Why Ethics Matters in a Machine-Driven World

When trades happen in microseconds, there's no pause to think, "Hmm, should I really do this?" By the time that thought forms, your algo has already sent, modified, and canceled 50 orders. That's why ethical decision-making has to happen before you deploy code, not in the middle of a live session.

Unethical but technically legal behavior erodes trust in markets. And trust, in finance, is like oxygen — you don't notice it when it's there, but you suffocate without it.

Ethical Grey Areas in Algo Trading

Exploiting Technical Glitches

- If your algo discovers a bug in an exchange's matching engine, do you use it for profit? The law may be murky, but the ethics aren't — exploiting system flaws can destabilize the market and harm others.

Predatory Strategies

- Some algos prey on slower participants in ways that, while legal, create an uneven playing field. For example, latency arbitrage against retail order flow.

Information Advantage

- If you're using alternative data, ask: was it obtained fairly? Scraping public websites is one thing; tapping into leaked or confidential data is another.

Market Impact

- Even a legal strategy can cause flash crashes or thin-market disruptions. Are you okay knowing your code might wipe out 3% of a stock's value in seconds?

Deceptive Design

- Building your algo to intentionally mislead other traders — even if it technically passes legal muster — is ethically questionable at best.

My Personal Code (and Why It's Saved Me Headaches)

Over two decades, I've boiled my own ethics checklist down to three rules:

1. Would I be comfortable explaining this strategy to a regulator in plain English?
2. Would I still run it if my mother saw a news article about it?
3. Would I trade against this algo if I were on the other side?

If I can't answer "yes" to all three, I go back to the drawing board. Simple, but it works.

Building Ethics Into Your Development Process

Code Reviews with a Compliance Mindset

- Have a second pair of eyes check for behaviors that could appear predatory or manipulative.

Simulate Market Impact

- Test how your strategy affects different participants, not just your own P&L.

Establish Internal Guidelines

- Write down what's off-limits for your shop — before temptation strikes.

Educate Your Team

- Make sure everyone involved understands not just the legal, but the ethical boundaries.

Closing Thought

At the end of the day, markets run on confidence. If algos become synonymous with manipulation, deception, or predatory behavior, regulators will clamp down harder, and everyone's opportunities shrink. Trading ethically isn't about being a saint — it's about ensuring the game stays worth playing.

And remember: the quickest way to ruin your reputation in trading is to be that trader whose code broke the market. It's hard to make friends at industry conferences when everyone remembers you as "the guy who accidentally crashed silver futures."

10.4 The Rise of AI and Its Implications

When I started in trading, "AI" meant a programmer had figured out how to make an Excel macro run without crashing. Now, AI has gone from a sci-fi buzzword to a full-blown participant in the markets — one that's faster, smarter, and occasionally more arrogant than its creators.

Artificial intelligence in algorithmic trading isn't just about automating tasks anymore. It's about giving machines the ability to adapt, predict, and learn from data in ways that make our old-school moving average crossovers look like toys. But with great computational power comes great... let's say opportunities to really mess things up.

How AI Is Changing the Game

Smarter Pattern Recognition

- AI models can detect subtle correlations and nonlinear relationships that traditional models miss.

- They can digest enormous datasets — news feeds, order books, sentiment scores — and turn them into trading signals in milliseconds.

Adaptive Learning

- Machine learning systems can update their parameters on the fly, adjusting to shifting market regimes.

- The good news: strategies stay relevant longer. The bad news: if the model "learns" the wrong lesson, it can self-destruct just as fast.

Alternative Data Integration

- AI thrives on messy, high-dimensional inputs: satellite images of parking lots, shipping data, weather patterns.

- The broader the data diet, the more complex the decision-making — and the harder it is to explain.

Autonomous Execution

- We're seeing AI handle not just what to trade, but how to trade it — adjusting execution styles in real time to minimize market impact.

Opportunities for Traders

Alpha Discovery

- AI can find inefficiencies human eyes would never spot — if the data quality is good enough.

Speed and Scale

- AI can scan hundreds of markets simultaneously without losing focus (try doing that before your second coffee).

Risk Management

- Advanced models can detect early signs of regime shifts or volatility spikes, acting as an early-warning system.

The Dark Side of AI in Trading

Black Box Risk

- Many AI models, especially deep learning, operate in ways even their creators can't fully explain. Regulators don't like "just trust me" as an audit trail.

Overfitting at Scale

- AI can overfit with style — finding patterns so specific they only work on the training set, and collapse in live trading.

Emergent Behavior

- Complex AI systems interacting in a market can create unexpected feedback loops — a fancy way of saying "flash crashes nobody saw coming."

Regulatory Uncertainty

- Most market abuse laws were written before AI trading was mainstream. The interpretation gap can cause legal headaches.

Ethical and Practical Implications

Accountability

- If an AI makes a bad trade, who's responsible? The developer? The firm? The algorithm itself? (Spoiler: the regulator will still call you.)

Transparency vs. Edge

- How do you explain your model without giving away the proprietary sauce?

Market Stability

- The more the market is run by self-learning agents, the higher the potential for correlated mistakes.

My AI Trading Rule of Thumb

Treat AI like a genius intern: give it the data, watch it work, but don't hand it the keys to the vault without supervision.

I've seen too many "autonomous" strategies burn through months of gains in an afternoon because the model decided a sudden price spike in nickel was "the new normal."

Closing Thought

AI in trading is here to stay, and the winners will be those who master the balance between innovation and control. The real risk isn't AI replacing traders — it's AI amplifying the mistakes of traders who don't fully understand what their own code is doing.

And remember, if your AI model ever becomes self-aware and starts asking for a corner office, you might have bigger problems than slippage.

10.5 The Future Landscape of Algorithmic Trading

If you think the current state of algorithmic trading is advanced, wait a few years — we're basically at the "flip phone" stage of what's coming. The pace of change in markets, data availability, and computing power is so fast that a strategy that's cutting-edge today might feel like dial-up internet tomorrow.

In two decades of watching markets evolve, I've learned one thing: the future doesn't arrive gradually. It shows up like a freight train, and if you're not already on the tracks with your strategy ready, you'll just be the guy waving as it passes.

Trends Shaping the Next Decade

Ubiquitous AI Integration

- AI won't be a novelty; it'll be the standard toolkit for everything from signal generation to trade execution.
- Expect hybrid human-machine decision systems, where AI crunches the numbers and humans provide the strategic oversight.

Explosion of Alternative Data

- We're moving past satellite images and social sentiment into real-time IoT sensor feeds, blockchain transaction networks, and biometric data from devices.
- The challenge won't be finding data, it'll be figuring out which bits of it actually matter.

Hyper-Personalized Strategies

- With increased computational capacity, firms will run thousands of micro-strategies tuned to specific assets, timeframes, and market conditions — all dynamically reweighted in real time.

Blockchain-Based Market Infrastructure

- Settlement times could drop from two days to seconds as blockchain and distributed ledger systems gain traction, which changes execution and risk models significantly.

Regulation-Driven Innovation

- As governments play catch-up with tech, new compliance rules will create both obstacles and opportunities. Traders who adapt quickly to new frameworks will thrive.

The Technology Arms Race

The days of competing purely on "better strategy logic" are over. The edge now often comes from how fast and how efficiently you can execute. Future competitive advantages will hinge on:

- **Quantum Computing (eventually)** — potentially solving complex optimization problems orders of magnitude faster than classical machines.

- **Edge Computing** — processing data closer to the source to cut latency.

- **Custom Silicon** — specialized chips designed for low-latency market calculations.

RISKS IN THE FUTURE Landscape

Systemic AI Correlation

- If most firms use similar AI models, the risk of everyone reacting the same way to a shock increases — potentially making flash crashes more violent.

Data Quality Arms Race

- Garbage in, garbage out will still apply, but now the garbage will be streaming in terabytes per second.

Geopolitical Data Wars

- Restrictions on cross-border data flows could impact the availability of key signals.

Regulatory Overcorrection

- A major market event triggered by algo misbehavior could lead to heavy-handed rules that slow innovation.

How to Stay Future-Proof

Continuous Learning

- Treat your tech and strategy stack as a living organism — keep evolving it.

Experiment in Sandboxes

- Simulate new tech and strategies in controlled environments before pushing them live.

Build Multi-Disciplinary Teams

- Tomorrow's trading desks will need quants, coders, data scientists, behavioral economists, and domain experts all in the same room.

Focus on Interpretability

- Black-box models are powerful, but if you can't explain them to a regulator or investor, you're already at a disadvantage.

Closing Thought

The future of algorithmic trading isn't about replacing humans with machines — it's about creating symbiotic systems where each does what it's best at. Machines handle the speed, scale, and statistical grunt work; humans handle judgment, ethics, and adaptability.

If you're prepared, the next decade could be the most exciting time ever to be in the markets. If you're not... well, let's just say you might end up telling stories about "the good old days" while your AI neighbor quietly trades options from its solar-powered yacht.

Let's face it—manual trading is exhausting. One minute you're riding high on green candles, the next you're doom-scrolling your portfolio and questioning every life decision since that "YOLO" trade. If that sounds familiar, you're not broken—you're just human.

That's where this book comes in.

The Art of Algorithmic Trading: Crafting Profitable Strategies is your no-nonsense (but slightly sarcastic) guide to transforming your chaotic trading journey into a systemized, data-driven, and semi-magical experience powered by cold, calculating code.

Across ten chapters packed with strategy, story, and a few mildly inappropriate jokes, you'll learn:

- How markets actually work (not just what influencers say)
- How to design trading strategies that aren't based on moon phases or vibes
- How to backtest like a scientist—not like an overconfident gambler
- How to manage risk so your bot doesn't accidentally try to short the S&P 500 into oblivion

And how to take your trading system live without it panicking and crying for its digital momma

You'll also dive into advanced techniques like statistical arbitrage, machine learning, and sentiment analysis—all without needing a PhD or sacrificing your social life (if you still have one after trading).

Whether you're a code-curious trader, a developer with market FOMO, or just someone who's tired of making emotional trades while yelling at candlestick charts like they're your ex—this book is for you.

A Note of Gratitude

If you've made it through this book, or even just read this far into the summary... thank you.

Seriously.

You could've spent your time watching cat videos or bingeing conspiracy theory documentaries on YouTube, but instead, you chose to dive into the wild world of algorithmic trading with me. That means a lot.

This book was written for curious, ambitious, slightly nerdy people like you—people who want to trade smarter, automate better, and maybe even laugh a little while doing it.

Thanks for trusting me to guide you through the chaos. I hope your future bots are profitable, your drawdowns are shallow, and your coffee is always strong.

Now go automate something awesome.

— *Talvek*

www.ingramcontent.com/pod-product-compliance
Ingram Content Group UK Ltd.
Pitfield, Milton Keynes, MK11 3LW, UK
UKHW020159290926
15471UKWH00005B/969

9 798231 548293